POLITICAL SCANDALS

OPPOSING VIEWPOINTS©

Other Books of Related Interest

POLITICAL SCANDALS

OPPOSING VIEWPOINTS©

William Dudley, *Book Editor*

David L. Bender, *Publisher*
Bruno Leone, *Executive Editor*
Bonnie Szumski, *Editorial Director*
Stuart B. Miller, *Managing Editor*

OPPOSING
VIEWPOINTS®
SERIES

Greenhaven Press, Inc., San Diego, California

Cover photo: Corbis

Library of Congress Cataloging-in-Publication Data

Political scandals : opposing viewpoints / William Dudley, book
   editor.
       p.   cm. — (Opposing viewpoints series)
   Includes bibliographical references and index.
   ISBN 0-7377-0517-5 (pbk. : alk. paper) —
ISBN 0-7377-0518-3 (lib. bdg. : alk. paper)
      1. Political corruption—United States. 2. Political ethics—
United States. I. Dudley, William, 1964–   . II. Series.

JK2249 .P648 2001
324.7'0973—dc21   00-029408
                                                                          CIP

Greenhaven Press, Inc., P.O. Box 289009
San Diego, CA 92198-9009

"Congress shall make no law...abridging the freedom of speech, or of the press."

First Amendment to the U.S. Constitution

The basic foundation of our democracy is the First Amendment guarantee of freedom of expression. The Opposing Viewpoints Series is dedicated to the concept of this basic freedom and the idea that it is more important to practice it than to enshrine it.

Contents

Why Consider Opposing Viewpoints?

*"The only way in which a human being can make some
approach to knowing the whole of a subject is by hearing
what can be said about it by persons of every variety of
opinion and studying all modes in which it can be looked
at by every character of mind. No wise man ever acquired
his wisdom in any mode but this."*

John Stuart Mill

In our media-intensive culture it is not difficult to find differing opinions. Thousands of newspapers and magazines
and dozens of radio and television talk shows resound with
differing points of view. The difficulty lies in deciding
which opinion to agree with and which "experts" seem the
most credible. The more inundated we become with differing opinions and claims, the more essential it is to hone
critical reading and thinking skills to evaluate these ideas.
Opposing Viewpoints books address this problem directly
by presenting stimulating debates that can be used to enhance and teach these skills. The varied opinions contained
in each book examine many different aspects of a single issue. While examining these conveniently edited opposing
views, readers can develop critical thinking skills such as the
ability to compare and contrast authors' credibility, facts,
argumentation styles, use of persuasive techniques, and
other stylistic tools. In short, the Opposing Viewpoints Series is an ideal way to attain the higher-level thinking and
reading skills so essential in a culture of diverse and contra-
dictory opinions.

In addition to providing a tool for critical thinking, Opposing Viewpoints books challenge readers to question
their own strongly held opinions and assumptions. Most
people form their opinions on the basis of upbringing,
peer pressure, and personal, cultural, or professional bias.
By reading carefully balanced opposing views, readers
must directly confront new ideas as well as the opinions of

those with whom they disagree. This is not to simplistically argue that everyone who reads opposing views will—or should—change his or her opinion. Instead, the series enhances readers' understanding of their own views by encouraging confrontation with opposing ideas. Careful examination of others' views can lead to the readers' understanding of the logical inconsistencies in their own opinions, perspective on why they hold an opinion, and the consideration of the possibility that their opinion requires further evaluation.

Evaluating Other Opinions

To ensure that this type of examination occurs, Opposing Viewpoints books present all types of opinions. Prominent spokespeople on different sides of each issue as well as well-known professionals from many disciplines challenge the reader. An additional goal of the series is to provide a forum for other, less known, or even unpopular viewpoints. The opinion of an ordinary person who has had to make the decision to cut off life support from a terminally ill relative, for example, may be just as valuable and provide just as much insight as a medical ethicist's professional opinion. The editors have two additional purposes in including these less known views. One, the editors encourage readers to respect others' opinions—even when not enhanced by professional credibility. It is only by reading or listening to and objectively evaluating others' ideas that one can determine whether they are worthy of consideration. Two, the inclusion of such viewpoints encourages the important critical thinking skill of objectively evaluating an author's credentials and bias. This evaluation will illuminate an author's reasons for taking a particular stance on an issue and will aid in readers' evaluation of the author's ideas.

As series editors of the Opposing Viewpoints Series, it is our hope that these books will give readers a deeper understanding of the issues debated and an appreciation of the complexity of even seemingly simple issues when good and honest people disagree. This awareness is particularly important in a democratic society such as ours in which people enter into public debate to determine the common good.

Those with whom one disagrees should not be regarded as enemies but rather as people whose views deserve careful examination and may shed light on one's own.

Thomas Jefferson once said that "difference of opinion leads to inquiry, and inquiry to truth." Jefferson, a broadly educated man, argued that "if a nation expects to be ignorant and free . . . it expects what never was and never will be." As individuals and as a nation, it is imperative that we consider the opinions of others and examine them with skill and discernment. The Opposing Viewpoints Series is intended to help readers achieve this goal.

David L. Bender & Bruno Leone,
Series Editors

Greenhaven Press anthologies primarily consist of previously published material taken from a variety of sources, including periodicals, books, scholarly journals, newspapers, government documents, and position papers from private and public organizations. These original sources are often edited for length and to ensure their accessibility for a young adult audience. The anthology editors also change the original titles of these works in order to clearly present the main thesis of each viewpoint and to explicitly indicate the opinion presented in the viewpoint. These alterations are made in consideration of both the reading and comprehension levels of a young adult audience. Every effort is made to ensure that Greenhaven Press accurately reflects the original intent of the authors included in this anthology.

Introduction

"It seems incontrovertible that political scandals have now acquired a prominent and important place in American political life."

British political scientist Robert Williams

Political scandals begin with various forms of wrongdoing by public officials. Money is often at the center of scandals in which politicians exploit their public office for private gain. Some scandals stem from acts of private misconduct, such as sexual misbehavior. Others involve abuses of government power that jeopardize people's rights and (in America) violate the U.S. Constitution.

However, mere wrongdoing is not enough to create a scandal. Scandals require public outrage and reaction, which in turn requires public disclosure. This is why, as Robert Williams notes in his 1998 study *Political Scandals in the USA*, countries with totalitarian or authoritarian political systems do not have scandals. "If the public are not allowed to know about the behaviour of politicians and officials, if they have no opportunity of voicing their concerns . . . , it is hard to see how scandals can arise," he argues. "Conversely, in a liberal political system with a free press, intense political competition, decentralized political authority and multiple access points, the opportunities and incentives for scandal to flourish are numerous."

Given this connection between disclosure, democracy, and scandal, it is perhaps not surprising that political scandals have been a recurrent feature of the American political scene since the administration of George Washington. However, while scandals have long been a part of American history, they seemed to have taken on an even more prominent role in American politics in the last quarter of the twentieth century. Scandals have brought about the resignation and disgrace of numerous powerful government officials and now seem to shadow almost everyone in public life. "In the past decade" wrote political journalist Joe Klein in 1998, "scandals . . . have become the defining events of public life, often far more compelling and significant than elections."

What accounts for the importance of scandals in current American politics? One possible answer is that the character of people in politics is worse than in earlier eras. However, many political observers believe that the current generation of leaders is no better or worse than previous generations; some, such as Klein, argue that Washington, D.C., is "far less corrupt than it has ever been." They argue that it is public awareness of scandalous activities that has grown. Two reasons for this are the changing role of the press and increased partisanship in Congress and the rest of government. Both developments are part of what has often been called the "post-Watergate" era. To understand contemporary political scandals requires a very brief explanation of what the Watergate scandal was and how it changed American society.

In 1972 the headquarters of the Democratic Party at the Watergate hotel complex in Washington, D.C., was burglarized. Subsequent investigations revealed that the burglars were connected to a group working for the reelection of Republican President Richard Nixon, and that Nixon, contrary to his public statements, found out about their involvement shortly after the incident and attempted to orchestrate a cover-up. The burglary was one of a series of "dirty tricks" Nixon and his subordinates used against political opponents, including the bugging of the Democratic National Committee and the misuse of government institutions such as the Central Intelligence Agency (CIA) and Federal Bureau of Investigation (FBI). Investigations also revealed that Nixon had solicited and received large secret cash contributions from individuals and corporations with a stake in government policies. Threatened with impeachment, Nixon resigned in 1974, the first and only U.S. president to do so.

Watergate had lasting ramifications on how politicians and scandals were treated by the press. The media—as well as the public—became more cynical about politicians and less willing to accept their statements at face value. The success and notoriety of *Washington Post* journalists Carl Bernstein and James Woodward for their part in exposing the Watergate scandal encouraged a subsequent generation of reporters to be aggressive in covering political scandals. In addition, the rise of the Internet, radio talk shows, and twenty-four-hour news channels has increased demand for such stories. One result has been more media coverage of matters formally considered private, including politicians' health, chemical abuse, and family issues. Incidents that would have remained gossip items among a few Washington journalists and insiders have now become grist for the media mill.

The political ramifications of Watergate—Nixon's resignation and the election of large numbers of Democrats to Congress—also left a lasting legacy. In subsequent years accusations of corruption and scandalous behavior have often become the weapon of choice in partisan political conflict. Political combatants have relied on personal attacks and accusations of scandal rather than debating substantive issues in order to secure an advantage. This tendency has been reinforced by the fact that, since 1980, control of the nation's government has been divided between political parties, with Republicans and Democrats alternating control of the presidency, Senate, and House of Representatives. Divided government has imparted a strong political tint to government investigations of scandal in the White House and in Congress.

The cases of Clarence Thomas and Bill Clinton are indicative of how scandals, especially those focusing on a person's character, can be interpreted as a byproduct of political infighting and media exposure. When Thomas was nominated to the Supreme Court in 1991 (to the consternation of many political liberals), his ratification hearings came to focus on accusations of sexual harassment from former employee Anita Hill. Sexual harassment was also at the center of a lawsuit filed against President Clinton (who was an anathema to many conservatives) in 1994 by former Arkansas state employee Paula Corbin Jones. Clinton's efforts to conceal a separate sexual affair with an intern, Monica Lewinsky, over the course of the Jones case formed the foundation of impeachment charges against him in 1998. In the cases of both Thomas and Clinton, lurid stories of sexual misconduct led to intense media scrutiny. Also in both cases, defenders of the two individuals argued that the accusations of scandal were being exploited for political reasons (the prevention of Thomas's accession, the removal of Clinton) to the detriment of America's system of government.

Whether the Thomas or the Clinton case will cause the public to seriously examine how scandals are viewed remains to be seen. The authors in *Political Scandals: Opposing Viewpoints* examine several key questions in the following chapters: How Serious Is the Problem of Political Scandals in America? How Relevant Is Private Morality to Public Office? Case Study: Was President Bill Clinton's Impeach ment Justified? What Reforms Can Prevent Political Corruption? The viewpoints will give the reader insight into the causes, ramifications, and possible solutions to the problem of political scandals in America.

CHAPTER 1

How Serious Is the Problem of Political Scandals in America?

Chapter Preface

In the democratic system of government in the United States, each person—rich, poor, or middle class—is entitled to one vote. Ideally, government officials are supposed to pass and enforce laws for the benefit of the whole community, without favoring one constituent over another. Unfortunately, politicians' currying favors for constituents in return for cash or other inducements is what lies at the heart of many political scandals.

Two examples from American history illustrate this classic form of political corruption. Warren G. Harding, president of the United States from 1921 to 1923, appointed friends to government positions who then used their position to benefit people in return for cash. His secretary of the interior, Albert Fall, took $400,000 in gifts and loans from oil millionaires Edward Doheny and Harry Sinclair while at the the same time leasing federal lands to them on favorable terms. More than half a century later, seven members of Congress were videotaped accepting cash and gifts from Arab oil sheiks (actually FBI officials in a sting operation) in return for promises to help them attain property, immigration visas, and other government favors. In both cases, the perpetrators were caught, convicted of bribery, and punished under the criminal justice system.

However, many people argue that today's politicians are being corrupted by money that is given to them in ways that are perfectly legal. The problem lies in the upwardly spiraling costs of running political campaigns (due largely to mass media advertising expenses). An estimated total of $2.2 billion was spent by candidates for all political offices in the 1996 elections. People running for local, state, and federal offices face the daunting prospect of raising thousands, even millions, of dollars each election cycle. They do so by seeking campaign contributions from individuals, corporations, labor unions, trade associations, and other groups. Some observers argue that donors gain access to tax breaks, regulation exemptions, and other special subsidies from the government. The viewpoints in this chapter examine the extent of corruption in government and the role of money in politics.

> "Corruption is rife in America, from the smallest communities to the West Wing of the White House."

Criminal Scandals Are a Serious Problem in U.S. Politics

Martin L. Gross

Martin L. Gross is the author of several nonfiction books, including *The Government Racket: Government Waste From A to Z*, *A Call for Revolution*, and *The Great Whitewater Fiasco*. The following viewpoint is an excerpt from his book *The Political Racket: Deceit, Self-Interest, and Corruption in American Politics*. Gross describes what he considers to be widespread corruption and unethical behavior in state and local governments as well as in Washington. Such corruption is countenanced by the political establishment that is more interested in personal enrichment than the public interest, Gross concludes.

As you read, consider the following questions:

1. What examples of criminal activity by members of Congress does Gross provide?
2. How many instances of political corruption does the author say happen annually in the United States?
3. What important principle was established in the California "sting" operations that Gross describes?

Excerpted from *The Political Racket*, by Martin L. Gross. Copyright ©1996 by Martin Gross. Reprinted by permission of Ballantine Books, a division of Random House, Inc.

Corruption is rife in America, from the smallest communities to the West Wing of the White House, whichever party occupies it. Apparently, it's not only because the profession seems to attract an outsize proportion of the unethical, but because the stakes are very high.

All governments in America—federal, state and local—spend $2.7 trillion a year, 40 percent of the entire GDP [gross domestic product], considerably more money than the Mafia ever dreamed of. There's enormous leeway in the decision as to who gets what portion of that enormous cornucopia. Naturally, both crooks and legitimate businessmen who want that tax exemption, that highway, that building permit, that government contract, *that everything*, will pay enormous sums to achieve their goals.

That's when politicians come into play. Their word, their encouragement, their bill, their committee staff influence, their friendly colleagues, can move millions (even billions) of dollars in one direction or another at the flick of a vote, or even an eyebrow. And they know it.

Among the ethical, it sets up a sense of enormous responsibility to do things fairly. Among the unethical, it's a chance for personal gain, especially cash. . . .

Corruption at HUD

Washington, in both the legislative and executive branch, is a pulsating center for both unethical behavior and corruption. One of the most heinous was the HUD (Housing and Urban Development) scandal of the 1980s, which showed that the agency was riddled with influence peddling and special deals that cost the taxpayers multi-millions of dollars.

An investigation by the House Committee on Government Operations issued a report on November 1990 that made the polemics of investigative journalists sound like a child's lullaby. Said the House report:

"During much of the 1980s, HUD was enveloped by influence peddling, favoritism, abuse, greed, fraud, embezzlement, and theft. In many housing programs, objective criteria gave way to political preference and cronyism, and favoritism supplanted fairness."

As the committee said, the rehabilitation program, "which

was intended for the poor, became a cash cow which was milked by former HUD officials and the politically well-connected.". . .

How Common Is Corruption?

Are the HUD scandals . . . just special incidents of political venality? Or is corruption rampant in America?

Are there perhaps fifty or so cases a year, aberrations in a generally moral environment? Are there a hundred cases a year? Surely not five hundred.

Try this: *The reality is that corruption by both elected politicians and government officials is epidemic.*

Criminal activity among members of Congress, for instance, far outweighs that of any other profession. Since 1970, thirty members of the House and Senate have been convicted of some type of criminal activity, ranging from racketeering to bribery to perjury to payroll padding to kickbacks to mail fraud to sex with minors to tax evasion.

In 1978, Representative Joshua Eilberg of Pennsylvania pled guilty to illegally taking money for services in which the federal government had an interest.

In 1979, Representative Charles C. Diggs admitted inflating the salaries of his staff so they could kick back money to pay his personal expenses. Subsequently, he was convicted of mail fraud and making false statements to the government.

Also in 1979, Representative Frederick W. Richmond of New York pled guilty to tax evasion, illegally supplementing the salary of a federal employee and possession of marijuana. He resigned from Congress.

In 1980, Representative Daniel Flood of Pennsylvania was charged with the "use of official influence on behalf of private parties and foreign governments in return for unlawful payments." He resigned and pled guilty.

In 1984, House member George V. Hansen of Idaho was convicted of making false statements to the government, the first violation of the Ethics in Government Act. He had failed to report $200,000 in loans and income and was sentenced to five months in prison. His defenders argued that he had been singled out for harsher punishment while others had committed similar transgressions.

In 1987, Representative Mario Biaggi of New York was convicted of accepting illegal gratuities, conspiracy and obstruction of justice, and was sentenced to jail. Then in 1988, he was convicted of bribery involving a Bronx, New York, defense contractor and sentenced to eight years in jail. In 1991, he was released from jail because of failing health.

In 1988, Representative Patrick L. Swindall of Georgia was convicted on nine counts of perjury for lying to a grand jury about trying to negotiate a loan from a drug-money launderer despite knowing that part of the proceeds was derived from the sale of illegal narcotics. He was sentenced to a year in jail and disbarred.

© Harley Schwadron. Reprinted with permission.

In 1990, Representative Albert G. Bustamente of Texas was convicted by a jury of accepting a $35,000 bribe from a food supplier for trying to get them a lucrative Air Force concession. His punishment? Three and a half years in jail and a substantial fine.

The Justice Department has established a Public Integrity Section, which tries to keep tabs on such crimes, or at least those prosecuted by federal authorities. Their latest "Report to Congress" (available to all citizens) is a wake-up call.

The annual total shows that 2,733 "Corrupt Public Officials," both elected and appointed, were convicted, indicted or awaiting trial during 1993 for crimes involving bribery, fraud, extortion or conflict-of-interest.

Since almost 3,000 public officials were actually caught in financial flagrante delicto, what should we assume? Probably that at least 10,000 such crimes are committed each year, a sad reflection on our body politic.

Political Crimes

The villains are greed and hubris. They stir up feelings among some politicians and officials that they are "special" people whose reward is the chance to exploit their office for privilege and benefits. That's not difficult considering the power we invest in our public officials. The difficult part for politicians is closing one's mind to personal gain, either for themselves or for friends, relatives and contributors.

But many can't resist the temptation, especially in the federal government, which won the 1994 corruption Olympics with 1,357 cases in one year.

The crimes range from venal bribery to padded government expense accounts to illegal conflict-of-interest. James L. Emery, former administrator of the St. Lawrence Seaway and onetime minority leader of the New York Assembly, pled guilty to charging Uncle Sam $9,128.28 for personal travel costs, and received five years of probation.

They involve ingenious schemes to defraud, some petty, others significant. In Hawaii, Marvin Miura, director of the state's Office of Environmental Control, took better care of himself than the environment. He received $35,000 in bribes in exchange for awarding no-bid contracts to friends, and was sentenced to thirty-three months in prison. . . .

Do the Justice Department lists show that political crime is decreasing or on the rise?

It seems to be a straight line upwards.

In 1974, the first year records were kept, there were a total of 523 cases convicted, indicted or awaiting trial. By the end of 1993, it had reached over 3,000. . . .

An Angry Public

The American public, finally, is in a heated reform mood and desperately wants cleaner government. There is a heightened awareness to match the declining morality of American politics and the billions raised and spent in campaigns. The mood is one which should be capitalized on immediately if we are to turn the tide. . . .

But surely bribery has nothing to do with your typical politician. He wouldn't think of taking cash for himself. Right? But he would take a campaign contribution, perhaps with the understanding that down the line he'd be doing a favor for the large contributor, even if it wasn't spelled out.

Isn't that the way the whole system works? Isn't that why a corporation will give a great deal of money to both parties—to protect some tax break or federal handout or ecological rule they need? That surely isn't criminal.

Don't be so sure about that.

Even without the bribe in the pocket, there may be the wink or the confidential handshake. We've always assumed that as long as a politician didn't directly take money for his own pocket, and though he might be guilty of unethical thoughts (so what's new?), at least he wasn't really a criminal.

Now a handful of prosecutors are asking the courts to stretch the definition of bribery and extortion, right into the world of campaign finance. They are not blindly accepting what is considered "normal" and "usual" in the raising of money. What used to be considered just a little shady or bordering on unethical in fund-raising may now be seen as criminal.

If the vote of the politician, or even his influence, was exchanged for an otherwise legal campaign contribution, it could be considered quid pro quo, and therefore a crime. (In Latin, it translates as "something for something," but in the American vernacular, it's perhaps best expressed as "you scratch my back and I'll scratch yours.")

That's a frightening thought that should make all politicians shudder.

2

| "Instead of debating issues of public policy,
| we focus more and more on allegations of
| personal wrongdoing—and deal with them
| not politically but by law and lawyers."

The Criminalization of Political Differences Is a Serious Problem in U.S. Politics

Anthony Lewis

Anthony Lewis is an award-winning columnist for the *New York Times*. In the following viewpoint, he argues that corruption in American politics was more common in the past than in the present. A more serious problem, he contends, is the tendency in American government to criminalize political differences and to be preoccupied with ethical appearances. Independent counsels (instituted by post-Watergate reforms to investigate government officials) have run amok in many instances in their zeal to prosecute government officials for relatively minor offenses, he asserts. In addition, the media highlights and exaggerates potential scandals as a way to attract audiences.

As you read, consider the following questions:
1. What examples of victims of overzealous investigations does Lewis describe?
2. How has the press changed since Watergate, according to the author?
3. How has the current preoccupation with investigating the ethics of public officials departed from the ideals of the nation's political founders such as James Madison, according to Lewis?

When Richard Holbrooke was chosen to be United States ambassador to the United Nations last June [1998], the State Department's inspector general received an anonymous letter charging that Holbrooke had violated ethics rules. The writer, who described himself as a department employee, said he based his charges on hearsay.

Over the next four months, agents of the State and Justice Departments investigated Holbrooke in this country and abroad. One subject was his failure to list as income, in his financial disclosure form, the use of a room in a friend's home in Washington when he was assistant secretary of state. Holbrooke had a real estate agent value the use of the room and amended the disclosure form to include the estimate, $12,000. The investigation focused finally on whether he had had improper contacts with U.S. diplomats after he left the job of assistant secretary in 1996 to become vice president of Credit Suisse First Boston. (He met with many diplomats on his frequent trips to Europe as special mediator on Cyprus.) The investigation was still going on when Holbrooke conducted his grueling negotiations with Slobodan Milosevic on Kosovo. Everyone knows that Richard Holbrooke is ambitious—but not for money. The Cyprus and Kosovo assignments were unpaid. His yearning is for what [former secretary of state] Dean Acheson called the "exhilaration" of public office. The notion that he would try to gain improperly from the use of a room in a friend's house is laughable, as is the idea that he had financial motives when he met American diplomats abroad. "We trust him to go over there and talk with Milosevic," a friend of his said, "but not to have dinner with someone. That is where the craziness with 'ethics' has taken us."

The Holbrooke episode is about more than an overdone preoccupation with ethics. It is indicative of a transformation in our politics. Instead of debating issues of public policy, we focus more and more on allegations of personal wrongdoing—and deal with them not politically but by law and lawyers.

The most dramatic example is of course the subjection of the president [Bill Clinton] to permanent investigation by a prosecutor whose power is limited only by his judgment, if any. But the phenomenon is far more pervasive than the behavior of Kenneth Starr. . . .

Nor is Kenneth Starr the only counsel who has made overzealous use of the Independent Counsel Act. Some of the other cases brought under the act are in their way just as indicative of the criminalization of our politics.

Criminalizing Politics

Henry Cisneros was President Clinton's first secretary of housing and urban affairs. He performed well in a difficult job, replacing bad public housing and making the department more efficient. But the wisdom of his policies and the effectiveness of his administration were not the business of the independent counsel who investigated him, David M. Barrett. In 1997, after he left office, Cisneros was indicted on 18 counts focused on the fact—much publicized in his home state, Texas—that he had a mistress. He told FBI agents about her when he was questioned before his nomination; but, the indictment charged, he understated what he paid her and for how long. He was also charged with lying when he told the agents that he had had no more than two extramarital affairs. Each of the 18 counts carries a maximum sentence of five years, so in theory Cisneros could go to prison for 90 years for what he did in connection with his sexual straying. To date, counsel Barrett has spent $7.3 million in pursuit of Henry Cisneros. [Editor's note: In September 1999 Cisneros pleaded guilty to one misdemeanor count of lying and paid a fine; the 18 felony counts were dropped.]

Mike Espy, the former secretary of agriculture, was indicted on 38 counts. He is charged, notably, with having accepted tickets to five football, basketball, and tennis events from companies that could be affected by Agriculture Department decisions. There is no claim that he actually did anything for the companies, and the law requires none. Even though some of the alleged "gratuities" are duplicated in different counts of the indictment, the total amount charged by the prosecution is $35,000. For this sum, Espy could go to prison for more than 100 years.

Donald Smaltz, the independent counsel in this matter, has spent $17.5 million so far trying to put Mike Espy away for his $35,000 sins. Along the way, he also had Sun-Diamond Growers of California, a raisin and nut cooperative, indicted for giving gifts to Espy. A jury convicted Sun-Diamond, and the company was fined $1.5 million; but a court of appeals reversed the conviction, ruling that the mere fact of gifts was not enough for conviction without proof of an intent to reward past favorable acts or make future ones more likely. . . .

The Espy case is a perfect example of the criminalization of politics. If it was wrong for a cabinet member to accept football tickets, the public could have handled it. In short, it was a matter that could have been dealt with politically—and in fact was. When the *Wall Street Journal* wrote about Espy's gift-taking in 1994, he resigned. But in addition to this, we have had a Smaltzian process that has dragged literally thousands of people into legal proceedings as witnesses or defendants. [Editor's note: Espy was acquitted by a jury of all corruption charges brought by Smaltz in December 1998.]

Starr's Chamber

Kenneth Starr's investigation raises unique problems because of its unique target. The Framers of the Constitution designed a system in which a single person embodied the executive branch. Put that person under continuous prosecutorial inquiry, and you inevitably weaken the presidency in the constitutional balance of powers. That was the central point made by Justice Antonin Scalia when he alone dissented from the Supreme Court's 1988 decision upholding the independent counsel concept. The Court's majority found that an independent counsel was an "inferior officer" subject to effective control by the president—a laughable notion in light of events—and hence did not offend the doctrine of the separation of powers. Justice Scalia's dissent reads now like a prophecy by Cassandra. "How easy it is," he wrote, "for one of the President's political foes . . . to trigger a debilitating criminal investigation of the Chief Executive under this law. . . . What if [the judges who appoint the counsel] are politically partisan, as judges have been known to be, and select a prosecutor antagonistic to the Administration . . . ?"

"What would normally be regarded as an investigation that has reached the level of pursuing such picayune matters that it should be concluded, may to [an independent counsel] be an investigation that ought to go on for another year." The point of having a single head of the executive branch, Justice Scalia said, was to make the president responsible politically—so that the public could hold the president accountable.

Politics and "Zero Tolerance"

Since the 1970s, criminal law has been reaching ever deeper into politics. The post-Watergate reforms brought a fine screen of campaign finance rules and, in 1978, the independent counsel law. The 1980s brought the "zero tolerance" prosecutorial mind-set, putting wetlands-fillers in jail with muggers and expelling students for bringing Advil or key-chain pocketknives to school. The result: a spectacular increase in prosecutions of public officials, stabilizing in the late 1980s at an unprecedented level (though dropping off a big in 1995). Through it all, the public became convinced that all politicians are crooked, if you only dig a little.

Politics is not like arson or battery, however. Politics is a messy affair, in which no two people will draw quite the same line between lobbying and peddling influence, or between rewarding supporters and paying them off. As zero-tolerance advanced, it was inevitable that at some point the ethics process would lose the ability to distinguish in any predictable way between politics and crime. That point has now arrived.

Jonathan Rauch, *National Journal*, March 14, 1998.

Impeachment was seen by [James] Madison and the other Framers [of the Constitution] as the ultimate political control over the president. But here again the process has been criminalized. Kenneth Starr acted as an agent of Congress for impeachment, using the terrible force of the criminal law. He had several grand juries as his instruments, with their power to compel testimony. And then he destroyed the one protection citizens do have, the secrecy of grand jury proceedings. President Clinton was treated as a criminal suspect—with fewer rights than any other.

These are just a few highlights of our progress toward a prosecutorial state. Richard Holbrooke is not the only official tormented by a lengthy ethics investigation over frivolous charges. Tony Lake and Sandy Berger, successive assistants to

President Clinton for national security affairs, were each investigated by the Justice Department for two years over stock holdings. Large numbers of state officials are now subjects of federal criminal inquiries. And civil litigation has become much more prosecutorial. If the price of shares in a young company falls, shareholders will sue, alleging that the drop is a result not of economic forces but of malefaction by company officials.

More Corruption than in the Past?

Has American leadership become more corrupt? By all accounts, wrongdoing by politicians was more common in the last century, whether nationally (the Grant Administration) or locally (the Tweed Ring). Nor can I believe that corporate or academic life is more laced with crime than it used to be. Something must have happened to us, the citizens, to make us more suspicious of our leaders, more eager to see them proved sinners.

Watergate is surely a proximate cause. I remember watching Nixon at the 1973 press conference when he said, "I am not a crook." Coming from a generation that regarded the presidency with instinctive respect, I was shocked. Subsequent disclosures—Nixon's use of thugs, the enemies' list, his anti-Semitic and locker room language, his attempt to have the CIA and FBI help cover up the Watergate break-in—went far toward destroying that presumption of respect.

Cynicism about public life has gone a long way since then. Polls showing contempt for officials are a familiar reality. Lloyd Cutler, who served in the Carter Administration and again in the Clinton White House, remarked on "the difference in the tone and virulence of the hate mail—and the frequency of four-letter words—not just toward the personality of the President but toward the White House itself and anyone foolish or crooked enough to work in the building."

Men and Angels

Watergate had a further consequence. After it was over, Congress passed the Ethics in Government Act, which institutionalized the idea of the independent counsel. Now, instead of special prosecutors being used by the attorney general as an ad hoc response to political problems—as was done at Teapot Dome and in Watergate—an elaborate process was set up to bind the attorney general. How constricting a process it is was made clear when Attorney General Janet Reno last May [1998] called for an independent counsel to investigate corruption charges against the secretary of labor, Alexis Herman. She did so, Reno wrote, "not because we possess affirmative evidence that Secretary Herman actually received money—we do not—but because we have not been able to answer all of the questions surrounding the alleged payments." In other words: in the absence of evidence, make the accused official bear the enormous financial and psychological burden of investigation by a counsel with no other object in life and no limitation of time or money.

The institutionalization of the independent counsel has had a profound political result as well. The demand for the appointment of a counsel has become the standard response to all kinds of issues. In campaign finance, for example, some people rightly exercised about abuses have devoted most of their energy to demanding a criminal investigation by an independent counsel rather than focusing on the need for changes in a financing system that invites abuse.

The search for purity has been a constant element in American history, expressed in recurring waves of liberal reform. Alas, reform can have unintended consequences. The substitution of a civil service regime for political appointments below the top level of government may have stopped the spoils system, but it has also made it hard to dislodge the lazy and incompetent. Some think the post office was more efficient, and less costly to customers, in the bad old political days. Former Senator Eugene McCarthy, writing in the *New York Times*, criticized the "current disposition to assign all difficult problems in American government to independent agents and procedures in which no elected official is held to account. By doing so, we have de-democratized much of government and criminalized much of politics."

There is a deeper cause, I think. Madison and the rest deliberately avoided creating a populist democracy, in which the mass of the public directly controlled government policy. They devised a representative republic, in which the judgment of the representatives would dampen the swings of public passion. But in recent years we have gone far toward a plebiscitary democracy in this vast country. Politicians look to polls and focus groups. Television has brought events into everyone's living rooms, and the public reaction tells officials what to do. The idea of actual leadership by men and women of wisdom seems hopelessly old-fashioned. Not many in Congress would say, as Edmund Burke did to his voters, "your representative owes you not his industry alone but his judgment, and he betrays instead of serving you if he sacrifices it to your opinion."

Changes in the Media

Change in the press has accelerated the populist trend. Think about the period after World War II. Scotty Reston of the [New York] Times, Walter Lippmann, and a few other columnists and editors prepared the way, by what they wrote, for the great shift from this country's historic isolationism to the embracing of international institutions: the United Nations, NATO, the IMF. To recall that kind of journalism now is to feel as if one is describing a distant century. Today we have a journalism seemingly governed by Gresham's law, with the cheapest and most vulgar driving others down to that level in order to compete. We have 24-hour cable television channels devoted in large part to condemnation of President Clinton's sex life. In the once more-serious broadcast networks we have the likes of George Will and Tim Russert and Sam Donaldson lecturing us on morality.

The press had a great moment in Watergate, when the reporting of Bob Woodward and Carl Bernstein led to the investigations by a Senate committee and by special prosecutors Archibald Cox and Leon Jaworski. The press's performance in publishing the Pentagon Papers—and generally in bringing home the reality of the Vietnam War—was another high achievement. But to a significant extent the serious work of investigating and analyzing large events has degenerated into "gotcha journalism," which aims to point fingers at sinners and demand their punishment.

There lurks in all of us a lust to see the great brought low. Scandal builds audiences—and sells advertising. So the television networks increasingly mimic the cable channels to feature scandal, while closing their news bureaus around the world. And our hunger for prosecutorial solutions to political problems grows apace.

The worst of it, for me, is the way the focus by the press and politicians on personal wrongdoings obliterates the distinction between the public and private spheres of life. Without privacy, [Czech writer] Milan Kundera wrote, "nothing is possible—not love, not friendship." Which of us would want to live in a situation in which nothing one said to a friend, a colleague, even a lawyer would be confidential—in which any one of them could be forced to testify against you? That is the life that Kenneth Starr has secured for presidents—that in addition to insisting that this president testify about an illicit sexual relationship and have the prosecutorial inquisition played on national television. . . .

Costs of the Prosecutorial State

The costs of the prosecutorial state are high. The loss of privacy, or even understanding the need for it, is one. The coarsening of society is another. A third is the disincentive it creates for people to enter public life. Anyone appointed to a significant job in the federal government now must undergo excruciating examination of his life, his finances, his friends, his medical history. And then, after appointment, he may be drawn into an investigation by an independent counsel or an antagonistic congressman. Whether he is a target or merely a witness, he will have to retain a private lawyer. He will pay the fees, and they are not likely to be modest. Lloyd Cutler, drawing on the experience of officials he has known, said in a speech that their legal fees amounted to as much as half their government salaries. He asked, "with these very high personal and financial costs, are there any mothers left who want their children to grow up to run for president or Congress or be appointed to executive office?"

There is also a question of simple justice. By now the institutionalized independent counsel system has damaged the lives of thousands of innocent individuals. When I wrote a column criticizing the indictment of Henry Cisneros, I received a telephone call from Raymond Donovan, who as secretary of labor in the Reagan administration was investigated by an independent counsel and cleared—but only after extended public humiliation. He agreed with my column, Mr. Donovan said, "though it comes a bit late to give me and my family comfort. I went to the public library recently with my latest grandson, who was doing a little paper. While I was waiting, I typed my name into a computer, and my knees went weak that my children and grandchildren would have to read such things."

The criminalizing of politics has a broader, more insidious impact. A decisive step in the development of free, self-governing polities was the acceptance of opposition as legitimate: the loyal opposition. Looking at less happy countries, we used to say that in democracies we could lose elections without losing our fortunes or our lives. But as our politics becomes criminalized, as we look for prosecutorial solutions to problems, partisan rancor and fear rise. The independent counsel process, Michael Walzer wrote in the *New Republic*, "became a kind of surrogate politics for people like me—and it has turned out to be a very bad politics. The legal process, set loose from its everyday constraints, will always turn up criminals. But what we should want, what democratic politics requires, are opponents.". . .

"If men were angels," Madison wrote in *The Federalist*, "no government would be necessary. . . . In framing a government which is to be administered by men over men, the great difficulty lies in this: you must first enable the government to control the governed; and in the next place oblige it to control itself." The Constitution's answer to the problem was political: a structure of balanced, competing powers answerable in the end to the people. Criminalization is a corrupting substitute for that structure. It seeks, vainly, to see to it that men are angels.

> "*Mammoth amounts of money have been
> poured into the political system by private
> interests which have thus purchased
> privilege, power and profit.*"

Money Has Corrupted the American Political System

Richard N. Goodwin

Business corporations and wealthy individuals have successfully purchased influence and votes in America's government through their financial contributions to political
officials and parties, argues Richard N. Goodwin in the following viewpoint. The enormous amount of dollars flowing into America's political system has corrupted it in favor
of those who contribute the most, he contends. Goodwin,
a former assistant to Presidents John F. Kennedy and Lyn-
don B. Johnson, argues for strict limits on political giving
and spending in order to remove the influence of "money
power" on government.

As you read, consider the following questions:
1. What great object of the Constitution has been nullified
   by money, according to Goodwin?
2. What sorts of favors do political contributors expect,
   according to the author?
3. What historical precedent does Goodwin cite as
   comparable with America's present political situation?

Reprinted from Richard N. Goodwin, "The Selling of Government Is a Scandal
Beyond Reform," *Los Angeles Times*, January 30, 1997, by permission of the author.

The great object of the new Constitution, James Madison wrote, was "to secure the public good and private rights against the danger of . . . faction." By "faction," Madison meant "a number of citizens . . . actuated by some common interest . . . adverse to the rights of other citizens or to the . . . interests of the community."

In recent years those constitutional protections have broken down. Mammoth amounts of money have been poured into the political system by private interests which have thus purchased privilege, power and profit. It would not be an exaggeration to assert that the American government—president, executive branch and Congress—has been bought and sold. Madisonian "faction" is firmly in the saddle and rides the nation.

We talk about this as if it were an issue of "campaign finance reform," an obscure and somewhat technical subject. But that is not the issue at all. It is not about how politicians should be financed, but how America should be governed, not about how we elect officials, but how they rule the nation.

Money Power

The principal power in Washington is no longer the government or the people it represents. It is the money power. Under the deceptive cloak of campaign contributions, access and influence, votes and amendments are bought and sold. Money establishes priorities of action, holds down federal revenues, revises federal legislation, shifts income from the middle class to the very rich. Money restrains the enforcement of laws written to protect the country from the abuses of wealth—laws that mandate environmental protection, antitrust laws, laws to protect the consumer against fraud, laws that safeguard the securities market, and many more.

The grotesque amounts of money that are now pouring into the political system and the disgusting and demeaning way in which that money is raised are testimony to mounting corruption of politics and of government. Much of this wealth is legally given. But the fact that one can wriggle through the loopholes of badly drafted laws does not amount to a moral justification or to a denial of corruption.

It has become customary for our derelict public officials to recite the mantra, "There was no quid pro quo" given to the contributor of great wealth. It is not only an absurd response, it is a lie. Does anyone really think that hundreds of millions of dollars are being poured into political campaigns out of an excess of public-spirited zeal? The reality is simply common sense: Most of those who give this money are making an investment—a business investment. And the return on this investment is huge. They cannot "buy a guaranteed result," President Clinton casually informs us. And in most cases that may be so. But that is not what they are purchasing. They are investing in access and influence, in the right to persuade or coerce elected officials to their point of view or to enlist the officials' support in disputes with the agencies of government. And they usually get what they pay for: influence over elected officials who pass the laws or control the agencies, who can open up opportunities or foreclose them, and—most important—influence their earnings and profits.

For both sides to this scandalous transaction there is a bottom line. For the politician it is measured in votes. For the

Cindy Frederick/LNS.

businessman the bottom line is profit and the protection of future earnings. No sensible businessman would deny himself so potentially profitable an investment, especially since experience demonstrates that you get what you pay for. And for both sides to the transaction there is also the reward of a nourished ego—the pride of being a high official cosseted by the titans of industry, or of being intimate with one of our guardians of democracy. It is a very comfortable arrangement in which everyone benefits except the people and the country.

We are amid corruption of a hitherto unknown scale but not without some precedent. In 1910, Bankers Magazine exulted that because of business financing of politics, "the legislatures and executive powers of the government are compelled to listen to the demands of organized business interests. That they are not entirely controlled by these interests is due to the fact that business organization has not yet reached its full perfection."

Take Money Out of Politics

In our time, perfection seems to have come a lot closer. But it may well be that the grotesque excesses of today will stimulate a serious reform. In the second decade of the 20th century, the Progressive movement responded to the conditions described by Bankers Magazine with protest, legislation and even a constitutional amendment requiring direct elections of the then totally corrupt Senate. The immediate issue is neither complicated nor difficult. But a little tinkering with "campaign finance laws,"as is now proposed, will once again prove a travesty. We need to take the money out of politics before money takes the politics out of politics. The way to do this is through unavoidable and Draconian limits on giving and spending.

Can it be done? Of course.

Will it be done? Not by our present officials, those who owe their office and power to the very system we seek to abolish. It will require today, as it has in the past, public protest and unrelenting exposure, a kind of national league against corruption, outside the parties and determined to drive from office all those who oppose reducing the power of wealth over our democracy.

*"Money talks, as it always will in a free
society. But in America, . . . strong
arguments can talk louder, and do."*

Money Has Not Corrupted the
American Political System

Michael Barone

Michael Barone, a political journalist and senior writer for
U.S. News & World Report, examines the role of money in
U.S. politics in the following viewpoint. He focuses on a
case chronicled by an October 1999 *New York Times* article
that described how a business executive successfully lobbied
for legislation governing asbestos lawsuits while heavily contributing to politicians and political parties. Barone rejects
the inference that this was an example of how money can
corruptly influence America's political leaders. He argues
that the enacted reforms had strong arguments in their favor, and that the executive was simply exercising his First
Amendment rights to lobby the government and express his
views. Money has a legitimate place in America's political
system, Barone concludes.

As you read, consider the following questions:
1. Who has espoused the argument that money buys
   legislation in America, according to Barone?
2. Who supported the reforms on asbestos lawsuits,
   according to the author?
3. What assertion does Barone make about the "general
   public interest?"

Reprinted from Michael Barone, "Money Talks, as It Should," *U.S. News & World
Report,* November 15, 1999. Copyright 1999, U.S. News & World Report. Visit us
at our website at www.usnews.com for additional information.

"How a company lets its cash talk," read the headline in the *New York Times* last month [October 1999]. The article tells of the success of Samuel Heyman, chairman of GAF Corp., in lobbying for a bill to change rules for asbestos lawsuits. The article sets out how much money Heyman, his wife, and GAF's political action committee have contributed to politicians and both parties, and the reader is invited to conclude that this billionaire and his company are purchasing legislation that will benefit them. Money buys legislation, which equals corruption: It is the theme articulated by John McCain in the Senate last month and on the campaign trail; . . . it is the mantra of countless editorial writers and of Elizabeth Drew in her book *The Corruption of American Politics.*

Strong Arguments Talk

But is it true? Careful readers of the *Times*'s "cash talks" story can find plenty of support for another conclusion: "Strong arguments talk." For 25 years, asbestos lawsuits have transferred billions of dollars from companies that once manufactured asbestos (it was banned in the 1970s) to workers exposed to asbestos and their lawyers. Asbestos causes sickness in some but by no means all workers many years after exposure. But most claimants who have recovered money are not sick and may never be, while those who are sick must often wait years for claims to be settled. The biggest winners in the current system are a handful of trial lawyers who take contingent fees of up to 40 percent and have made literally billions of dollars.

Heyman's proposal, altered somewhat by a proposed House compromise, would stop nonsick plaintiffs from getting any money, while setting up an administrative system to determine which plaintiffs are sick and to offer them quick settlements based on previous recoveries. The statute of limitations would be tolled, which means that nonsick plaintiffs could recover whenever signs of sickness appear. Sick plaintiffs would get more money more quickly, while companies would be less likely to go bankrupt; 15 asbestos firms are bankrupt now, and the largest pays only 10 cents on the dollar on asbestos claims. The two groups who lose, according to Christopher Edley, a former Clinton White House aide and Harvard Law professor who has worked on the legislation, would be nonsick plaintiffs who might get some (usually small) settlements under the current system and the trial lawyers who have been taking huge contingent fees.

Too Much Money?

If fund raising continues at the current pace, candidates for the House, Senate and presidency will spend $3 billion in the 1999–2000 cycle, an $800 million increase over the 1995–96 presidential election cycle. But to put that $800 million—in eight quarters—in perspective: $655 million was spent on advertising on the Internet in just the last quarter of 1998.

That $3 billion would come to $14.60 per eligible voter for political communication about the determination of public policy—about the presidential contest, 435 House contests and 34 Senate contests. Too much? By what standard?

George F. Will, *Sacramento Bee*, October 10, 1999.

These are strong arguments, strong enough to win bipartisan support for the bill, from Democratic Sens. Charles Schumer and Robert Torricelli as well as House Judiciary Chairman Henry Hyde and Senate Majority Leader Trent Lott. You would expect Hyde and Lott to support such a law, but for Schumer and, especially, Torricelli, it goes against political interest: Torricelli chairs the Senate Democrats' campaign committee, and Democrats depend heavily on trial lawyer money. One can only conclude that Schumer and Torricelli were convinced by strong arguments, which was certainly the case for Democrat Edley, who was writing about cases long before Heyman's bill was proposed. When McCain charged that the current campaign finance system was corrupt, Republican Mitch McConnell challenged him to name one senator who had voted corruptly. Certainly no one who knows the issues and the senators involved would have cited this case.

Air Pollution?

And not just this case. When a government affects the economy, when it sets rules that channel vast sums of capital, people in the market economy are going to try to affect government. They will contribute to candidates and exercise their First Amendment right to "petition the government for a redress of grievances," i.e., lobby. Both things will continue to be true even if one of McCain's various campaign finance bills is passed. There is no prospect for full public financing of campaigns . . . ; one reason is that it leaves no way to prevent frivolous candidates from receiving public funds. (Look at the zoo of candidates competing for the Reform Party's $13 million pot of federal money.) Reformers speak of campaign advertisements as if they were a form of pollution and try to suppress issue ads as if no one but a candidate (or newspaper editorialist) had a First Amendment right to comment on politicians' fitness for office. And to communicate political ideas in a country of 270 million people you have to spend money.

The idea that the general public interest goes unrepresented is nonsense. There is no single public interest; reasonable people can and do disagree about every issue, from asbestos lawsuits to zoo deacquisitions. This country is rich with voluntary associations ready to represent almost anyone on anything; any interest without representation can quickly get some. Even when the deck seems stacked, as it has for trial lawyers on asbestos regulation, there will be a Samuel Heyman with, as Edley puts it, "the moxie to act on his convictions." Money talks, as it always will in a free society. But in America, and on Capitol Hill, strong arguments can talk louder, and do.

Periodical Bibliography

The following articles have been selected to supplement the diverse views presented in this chapter. Addresses are provided for periodicals not indexed in the *Readers' Guide to Periodical Literature, the Alternative Press Index*, the *Social Sciences Index*, or the *Index to Legal Periodicals and Books*.

Kevin Clarke	"Government for Hire?" *U.S. Catholic*, July 1999.
Brian Doherty	"Common Causes," *Reason*, April 1996.
Ann Reilly Dowd	"We Now Have a Vested Interest in Scandal," *Columbia Journalism Review*, July/August 1997.
David Grann	"Espy and the Criminalization of Politics," *New Republic*, February 2, 1998.
Marty Jezer	"Soft Money, Hard Choices: A Primer on Campaign Finance Reform," *Dollars & Sense*, July 17, 1996.
Joseph Lieberman	"A Republic—If We Can Keep It," *Atlantic Monthly*, July 1998.
Tod Lindberg	"Money and Politics," *Policy Review*, August/September 1999.
Charles Mahtesian	"The Ethics Backlash," *Governing*, October 1999.
Jeff Milyo	"Money Walks: Why Campaign Contributions Aren't as Corrupting as You Think," *Reason*, July 1997.
John Mueller	"Well Off," *New Republic*, November 15, 1999.
Jonathan Rauch	"Guilty of Politics," *National Journal*, March 14, 1998. Available at www.nationaljournal.com.
Frank Rich	"The Donor Class," *New York Times*, July 19, 1998.
Robert J. Samuelson	"The Price of Politics," *Newsweek*, August 28, 1995.
David M. Stone	"Still in Watergate's Shadow," *Tikkun*, September/October 1999.
Michael Wines	"Supreme Leader, Pigeon in Chief," *New York Times*, March 23, 1997.

CHAPTER 2

How Relevant Is Private Morality to Public Office?

Chapter Preface

As president, John F. Kennedy cultivated his image as a devoted family man with a glamorous wife and two children. In recent years, his legacy has been tarnished by revelations that he had numerous sexual affairs. Kennedy's escapades were known to many journalists and associates, but in that era such information was not revealed to the general public.

The media has since changed in how it reports on the private lives of politicians. A candidate's history regarding sex, drug abuse, and other "private" matters is commonly placed under intense media scrutiny. A turning point came in 1987 when Gary Hart was forced to drop out of the presidential race because of revelations of an adulterous relationship. In 1992, Arkansas governor Bill Clinton took the unusual step of admitting on national television that he had "caused pain in [his] marriage." With the support of his wife Hillary, Clinton was able to overcome his admission and be elected president in 1992 and again in 1996.

In 1997 the Supreme Court ruled that a sexual harassment lawsuit by Paula Jones (concerning an incident that occurred while Clinton was governor) could go forward. In a January 1998 deposition, lawyers for Jones, seeking supporting evidence for their case, asked the president whether he had sexual relations with Monica Lewinsky, a former White House intern. Clinton denied that allegation both in his deposition and to the American public when the sensational story became publicized. However, months later in August 1998, after Clinton independent counsel Kenneth Starr obtained DNA evidence and sworn testimony from Lewinsky, Clinton admitted to a federal grand jury and to the American public that he and Lewinsky had an "inappropriate intimate relationship." Clinton's earlier denials became part of the basis for his subsequent controversial impeachment by the House of Representatives in December 1998.

Clinton's troubles brought to the forefront the question of how private character relates to political leadership. The authors in this chapter debate whether the public should be greatly concerned about politicians' private lives.

"We are not compartmentalized beings whose private selves are somehow divorced from our public selves."

There Is a Direct Connection Between Public Leadership and Private Morality

Leslie Carbone

Leslie Carbone is a policy analyst at the Family Research Council, a conservative research and educational organization. In the following viewpoint, she makes several arguments on why a political leader's personal character is important in evaluating his or her public record. For example, she contends that a person who disregards marriage vows cannot be trusted as a politician to honor public commitments or be a good role model. The fact that there is a debate over the link between public and private morality indicates that the United States is in a moral crisis, she asserts.

As you read, consider the following questions:

1. What reasons does Carbone give for her contention that "character counts"?
2. What disturbing public opinion trend, in Carbone's view, was revealed by a Gallup poll?
3. What possible harmful public policies may be pursued by immoral political leaders, according to the author?

Reprinted from Leslie Carbone, "Why Character Counts," article on the website of the Family Research Council at www.frc.org. Used by permission of the Family Research Council, Washington, D.C.

E very now and then, a debate emerges over a question to which the answer is so obvious that the mere existence of the debate reveals that our society is in serious moral crisis. Such is today's debate over whether a leader's character matters.

Character Counts

Yes, character counts. Character counts because it is the framework within which we do everything we do. We are not compartmentalized beings whose private selves are somehow divorced from our public selves. Those who lack honor in private will lack honor in public. We don't change who we are when we go to work.

Character matters in a leader because those who seek and exhibit wisdom, prudence, and discipline in their private lives are more likely to seek and exhibit these virtues in their public roles. Developing them requires time, commitment, practice, and a desire to do right. One who has not made them a priority in private life will not have them to draw upon in executing public responsibilities.

A leader's character matters because it is impossible to separate leadership from example. When a leader is morally depraved, the people—especially children—learn that depravity is acceptable, perhaps even rewarded.

Character counts because it determines the consequences that one will reap in one's own life, which can become distractions from one's public role. Do we really want a leader trying to figure out how to placate his wronged wife while negotiating arms agreements? Do we want his advisors spending time concocting plausible alibis for him instead of seeking solutions to national problems?

Character determines what we do, how we make decisions, how we treat others, and how we respond when the going gets tough and when the going is great. These are the issues that are central to leadership.

American Voters

Unfortunately for the country, a majority of voters don't recognize this. A 1998 Gallup poll found that 65 percent of Americans say that they do not need to know whether a presidential candidate has had extramarital affairs in order to evaluate him. These voters are rejecting a critical factor in determining what kind of leader a candidate will be. How can they even be sure that he'll do what he says he'll do once in office? Why would he honor promises made on the campaign trail if he won't honor his marital vows made before God?

Even beyond the personal strengths and weaknesses that a leader will bring to his job day after day, his character raises questions and points to the answers about the values he will bring to the specific decisions he'll make.

Decisions on Values

If a candidate bears little regard for his own marriage, will he evaluate public policy with properly critical concern for how it will impact yours? Will he object to domestic partner benefits that raise homosexual relationships to the level of marriage if he doesn't value the sanctity of marriage in the first place? Will he object to a tax that undermines marriage and encourages cohabitation?

Infidelity and Trust

Infidelity primarily is about lying. That is why it is incorrect to assert that a politician, or anyone else, can be one person in his or her "public life" and another person in private. If one lies about a marital promise, on what basis do we judge his standard for telling the truth elsewhere?

Cal Thomas, *Dallas Morning News*, May 24, 1997.

If a candidate chooses the short-term pleasures offered by adulterous flings over the faithfulness, discipline, and plain hard work that reap the long-term reward of a great marriage, will he then also choose public policies that offer quick fixes, with little or no regard for their long-term consequences? Will he be likely to favor a tax increase to resolve a deficit, leaving the resulting economic damage for his successors to address? Will he favor employment quotas to placate a vocal group of homosexuals, without considering whether they will force day care centers to hire pedophiles?

If a candidate is unwilling to practice self-denial in his own life, will he favor policies that expect equally poor discipline of the citizenry? Will he be likely to favor public condom distribution programs on the grounds that children can't be expected to rein in their passions any more than he can? Will he endorse public needle- and drug-giveaway programs, since cleaning up and staying drug-free is just too hard for some?

If he views women as sex objects, can he properly evaluate policies that impact us? Will he support appropriately harsh penalties for rape, or just assume that rape victims ask for it?

If a leader has no qualms about having a sexual relationship with a subordinate, wouldn't he be likely to misuse power in other ways? Would he take advantage of power to access his opponents' confidential files? Will he really care that much about IRS abuses of the "little people"? Will he nominate judges who trample our Constitutional rights? Will he encourage the unbridled growth of state power over every aspect of our lives?

Decisions are made according to one's values, and values are revealed by character. A leader who treats his own family shabbily is unlikely to treat yours any better. One who does not value honor and discipline in himself is unlikely to value them in others. One who abuses power for personal pleasure will abuse power for political gain as well. The results will be policies that undermine the family, punish character, reward depravity, and expand government. These in turn will destroy any society.

Character determines the daily decisions that set the course of a life, a family, or a nation. Good leadership depends on good character. Character counts.

"Private misdeeds are perfectly consistent with a good, even outstanding, public record."

There Is No Direct Connection Between Public Leadership and Private Morality

John B. Judis

John B. Judis is a senior editor of the *New Republic* magazine. In the following viewpoint, written when the U.S. Senate was debating the impeachment of President Bill Clinton for offenses related to a sexual affair, Judis examines the case of David Lloyd George, Great Britain's prime minister from 1916 to 1922. He argues that although Lloyd George was plagued by financial and sexual scandals, he achieved a note-worthy public record as prime minister, including leading Great Britain to victory in World War I. His example demonstrates that a person's private misdeeds can coexist with an outstanding public career, Judis concludes.

As you read, consider the following questions:
1. Adulterous affairs were not usually publicized in Lloyd George's time except in what case, according to Judis?
2. What parallels does Judis see between Lloyd George and Bill Clinton?
3. What conclusions does the author draw about Congress and impeachment?

With every day, Congress seems closer to censuring the president—and further from removing him altogether—on the grounds that his misdeeds don't rise to the level of a constitutional crime. But even a decision to slap Bill Clinton with an official reprimand would implicitly endorse one of the most dangerous arguments behind the impeachment drive: that there is a seamless moral web between a politician's private acts and his performance as a public official. So, before Congress considers such a measure, it would do well to consider yet another powerful historical example—one that has not yet entered the dialogue over President Clinton's fate. That example is David Lloyd George, one of Britain's greatest national leaders.

A Great Prime Minister

Lloyd George was responsible not only for enacting Britain's social insurance system but also for liberating Parliament and British democracy from vetoes by the House of Lords, which Lloyd George described as "five hundred men, chosen accidentally from the unemployed." After taking over as prime minister in 1916, he led a demoralized Britain out of a military stalemate to victory in World War I. Winston Churchill wrote of him: "When the English history of the first quarter of the twentieth century is written, it will be seen that the greater part of our fortune in peace and war were shaped by this one man."

Lloyd George was the first "ranker" of humble origin to become prime minister. When he was only 18 months old, his father died, and he was raised in a Welsh village by his mother, his grandmother, and his uncle, a shoemaker. He was educated by an Anglican schoolmaster but had to be helped by his uncle to prepare for the difficult examination to become a lawyer. In 1890, he was elected to Parliament as a Liberal. He was strikingly handsome and a mesmerizing orator who had, one London editor commented, "the swiftest mind in politics." The French ambassador wrote that he was "a Welshman, not an Englishman . . . enthusiastic, bright, quickwitted, and unsettled." His detractors invariably described him as a "demagogue" lacking in fixed convictions, but in retrospect he stands out as a founder of modern British and American liberalism.

The Virtues of Hypocrisy

For the sake of public morality, we need to return to something resembling the old arrangement whereby the press largely kept quiet on the subject of politicians' sex lives. Paradoxically, while this will give some politicians a free pass, it will, at the same time, enhance public morality, which is more important. . . .

Politicians serve as role models. By fudging the full facts of, for example, JFK's dalliances, the press presented a picture to the American people of what a family should be. In so doing, it gave inspiration to everyday citizens to practice the good morals that help families prosper.

Were politicians such as JFK hypocritical in such a display? Of course. And perhaps the media were no less guilty of being enablers of this hypocrisy. But, while unattractive, is hypocrisy necessarily the worst of human traits? Consider the insight of the 17th-century French writer, La Rochefoucauld, who described hypocrisy as "the tribute vice pays to virtue." By this he meant that a certain degree of hypocrisy must both be accepted and can even be salutary for public morality. Think about the alternatives to hypocrisy: sainthood or shamelessness. The former always is in short supply. It is the stuff of angels. The latter, many will agree, is becoming a growth stock. . . .

Hypocrisy serves virtue because if it does not take virtue seriously enough to practice it privately, it at least promotes virtue through publicly paying it lip service. In the vale of tears that is this world, when the culture can keep its fallen members in line at least to the extent that they publicly support morality, that's not so bad.

Thomas K. Lindsay, *Insight*, October 12, 1998.

Plagued by Scandals

Lloyd George was, however, plagued by scandals—primarily of his own making but also magnified by his Tory opponents in Parliament and in the press. From his first days in Parliament, when officials were still not paid, he augmented his income through questionable means. The most embarrassing occurred in 1912 when he was chancellor of the exchequer. Lloyd George and other government officials bought privately offered shares in the wireless company American Marconi at a time when the government was negotiating with British Marconi to establish radio communications throughout the British empire. The two companies were legally separate, but British Marconi was the majority shareholder in the American firm. The Tories attacked him mercilessly for insider trading. The scandal raged for months, although it made no impact outside of London. After an investigation controlled by the Liberals cleared the government, the Tories demanded a vote of censure, but it failed. Lloyd George, who ended up losing money on the investments, declared disingenuously during the censure debate: "I am conscious of having done nothing which brings a stain upon the honor of a minister of the Crown. If you will, I acted thoughtlessly, I acted carelessly, I acted mistakenly, but I acted innocently, I acted openly, and I acted honestly."

Lloyd George, who was married in 1888 and had five children, was also known as a philanderer. Back then, politicians' adulterous affairs were not usually publicized and did not threaten their careers unless they resulted in divorce. In 1897, however, Lloyd George reportedly had to bribe an irate husband from naming him in a divorce suit. Then, in 1909, in the midst of the climactic battle over the "People's Budget," People, a London tabloid, suddenly revealed that he had bought his way out of being named in yet another divorce suit. This time, he sued the newspaper for libel, and he and his wife testified falsely that its report of an affair and payoff was an "absolute invention." His eldest son later recounted the conversation between Lloyd George and his wife, Margaret:

> He knew that he would be attacked mercilessly if my mother expressed open doubt as to his innocence, if it were shown that she did not support him in his rejection of the accusation. . . . I know that my mother, a deeply religious woman, was in torment in giving support to the lie to be sworn on oath. . . . "You must help me, Maggie. If I get over this, I give my oath you shall never have to suffer this ordeal again." . . . "How can I rely on your oath?" "I can make it true, Maggie, I put my life in jeopardy for my beliefs. One day I shall be prime minister. I shall be a force for the public good. If you help me, you shall never regret your decision."

As a result of his and his wife's false testimony, he won a judgment against People, which he donated to a Welsh charity. Four years later, Lloyd George, who was 49, fell in love with Frances Stevenson, his daughter's 24-year-old tutor, and made her his private secretary and mistress. They were married 30 years later, after Lloyd George's wife died. So much for fidelity and honesty in one of Britain's greatest prime ministers.

There are, of course, striking similarities between Lloyd George and Bill Clinton, from their modest upbringing to their political style (Lloyd George was also known as a great "reconciler" for his ability to settle conflicts) to Marconi and Whitewater and People and Monica Lewinsky. Bill Clinton is unlikely to be remembered as one of the century's great presidents, but that is not because he lacked ability; he didn't have the political support to pass an ambitious agenda.

Private Character and Public Record

Either way, the moral is the same: just as sterling private character doesn't guarantee great leadership, private misdeeds are perfectly consistent with a good, even outstanding, public record. Yes, public officials can become deranged and commit heinous private acts that merit their immediate removal. But, as the nation's founders recognized, and as the public has understood from the beginning of this scandal, Congress should narrowly circumscribe its purview to include acts committed in an official capacity. It should leave to conscience, the courts, and the court of public opinion acts of adultery (even when falsely denied in court) and financial irregularities that don't arise from the pursuit of or conduct in public office.

> *"The idea of more openness by politicians regarding their private lives is not an inherently bad one."*

Greater Public Exposure of the Private Lives of Politicians Would Benefit America

Gary L. Bauer

In the following viewpoint, Gary L. Bauer argues that politicians should be subject to greater public disclosure of their private lives in order to ensure that the nation's leaders are people of good character. The country depends on its leaders to uphold high moral standards and to acknowledge and learn from past mistakes, he contends. Voters should have the right to know what kind of personal background political candidates possess before electing them. Bauer is a former domestic policy adviser to President Ronald Reagan and president of American Renewal, a conservative advocacy organization.

As you read, consider the following questions:
1. What examples of public leaders who have revealed private indiscretions does Bauer describe?
2. What point does the author make concerning the argument for full disclosure of campaign contributions?
3. What impact might the Clinton scandals have on the future of the American presidency, according to Bauer?

There are reports that, in response to the scrutiny that President Clinton has faced concerning his private life, the White House will disseminate information about the private lives of other public figures, such as the congressmen who may decide whether to draft articles of impeachment. In anticipation of such a smear campaign by the White House, House Government Reform and Oversight Committee Chairman Dan Burton of Indiana disclosed that he had fathered an illegitimate child.

Burton had the courage to admit a past failing rather than be held hostage by it. Although we must decry any attempt to intimidate or spread false information, the idea of more openness by politicians regarding their private lives is not an inherently bad one. When the dialogue is conducted respectfully it is good for the public to desire a high standard of morality from its leaders, and it is good when politicians speak openly on this issue rather than attempt to cover up past moral failings.

Privacy and Responsibility

Politicians already know that when they enter public life, they sacrifice almost all of their privacy. Although leaders should have some level of privacy because they are human like the rest of us, too often the mantle of privacy is used as a way of avoiding accountability.

Privacy has become a synonym for moral relativism and radical individualism. It is no coincidence that invented privacy rights are used to perpetuate one of our culture's most destructive tendencies—abortion. Now President Clinton has tried to claim a zone of privacy that would undermine the rule of law.

One might argue that disclosure is useless because the public knew of Clinton's moral weaknesses, yet elected him twice. However, it is precisely because President Clinton's failings have been revealed through the Monica Lewinsky scandal that the public is becoming aware of the weight of character flaws they once ignored. Disclosure about candidates is helpful, but it cannot be effective without citizens making moral distinctions on the basis of what is disclosed.

The founders of our country knew that a democracy

could not prevail without standards of morality. They also knew that government teaches its citizens lessons about morality. Therefore they emphasized the need for strong character as a requirement in leaders. The goal of increased disclosure by candidates regarding their private lives is to elect people of good character—not to set unrealistic standards of perfection for our leaders. The Bible says that all of us have sinned. Without a doubt, I place myself in that category. If perfection in leaders were required, we would never have any. The best leaders are not the ones who pretend not to have flaws, but those who learn from their flaws. There are examples of outstanding leaders who have acknowledged grave mistakes and become better people afterward.

Rising Above Past Mistakes

Some supporters of President Grover Cleveland probably thought that he was making his 1884 presidential campaign overly difficult when he acknowledged fathering a son out of wedlock with Maria Halpin. Because no proof of paternity existed, Cleveland could have sought refuge in the gray areas by trying to pin the responsibility on others. Instead, he claimed the child, paid child support and arranged for his adoption. For his candor, Cleveland received chants from his opponents: "Ma, Ma, where's my pa? Gone to the White House, ha, ha, ha!" But Cleveland was elected and went on to take a strong and principled stand against pet government programs. Marvin Olasky has brought attention to President Cleveland as an example of a leader who acknowledged his moral failure, made amends and went on to serve the country with good character.

In 1976, J.C. Watts, now a Republican congressman from Oklahoma, also fathered a child out of wedlock. Afterward, he became a youth pastor and used the lessons from that experience to teach teens not to make the same mistake. He says that he is proud of the fact that, "I took a bad situation and made a very, very positive situation out of it." Now he has become a rising star in the House who has supported federal spending cuts, welfare reform and more power to parents. "Redemption is a farce if you can't be forgiven for your mistakes," Watts says.

Full Disclosure

Why doesn't the logic of full disclosure for the source of campaign funding apply equally well to the personal backgrounds of politicians who want to wield public power? People on both sides of the campaign-finance debate generally agree that increased disclosure of campaign contributions would give more opportunity to see who is giving money to candidates so that voters can make the best decision about whom they want in office. More disclosure of campaign contributions is a good idea. As Justice Louis Brandeis has said, "Sunlight is the best disinfectant."

The Legacy of the Clinton Scandal

When Gary Hart left the race for the Democratic presidential nomination in 1987 after being caught in an extramarital dalliance, public talk was about Donna Rice spending the night in his apartment and sitting on his lap on a yacht named Monkey Business.

In 10 years, discussion has gone from merely implied mentions of sex to very specific kinds of sex, noted Democratic strategist Mark Mellman of Washington. "It will be hard to put the genie back in the bottle," he said.

Many analysts, in fact, say the biggest effect of the Clinton scandal is a broader definition of fair game in politics.

"The boundaries of what constitutes corruption and misconduct in public life have been redrawn to include a lot more private conduct," said Michael Johnston, a Colgate University professor who has studied scandals for two decades.

What the scandals are about may change, he said, but "we're increasingly substituting scandal for politics."

Carolyn Barta, *Dallas Morning News*, February 13, 1999.

The same is true for a candidate's character. As important as it is for voters to know what kind of financial capital a candidate is drawing from in a bid to serve the public, it is even more important that voters know what kind of moral capital a candidate is drawing from. Just as we don't want public officials who are dominated by their ties with special interests, we don't want officials dominated by their greed, lust or arrogance. In fact, knowing character is more important than knowing about contributions, because it is corruption *inside* a person that fuels corruption on the outside.

Public Consequences

In recent months, we have seen the consequences of uncontrolled personal appetite in our president. Although such appetites generally begin in private, they have public consequences. Moreover, President Clinton's reckless betrayal of his wife rightly colors the way we look at the decisions he has made regarding the public good. For instance, we wonder whether we can trust him when he defends his decision to relax the standards on sharing technology with China. The same person who makes the private decisions makes the public ones. It is absurd to pretend that a leader's public and private lives are entirely separate. Hiding the bad news about one's past often causes more trouble than disclosing it.

President Clinton is in more danger now than he was when the Lewinsky revelations first came out because of his attempts to hide the matter by lying to the nation. His cover-up has backfired with his fellow Democrats, who now feel a sense of betrayal in addition to the disappointment felt by the American public. . . . Furthermore, by claiming all sorts of legal privileges the courts resoundingly rejected, President Clinton may have damaged the office of the presidency for years to come.

Although the Lewinsky matter has caused a lot of damage, it also may cause Americans to raise their expectations for the character of future occupants of the White House. This would be a good development for the presidency. At the same time, fuller disclosure of the backgrounds of congressmen and senators would allow voters to make more-informed decisions for those offices as well. It isn't necessary to turn politics into a witch-hunt in which unrealistic moral standards are arbitrarily enforced. Americans must instead use reasonable moral standards to protect the honor of their government and the hopes of their children. If they do so, they can bring renewed health to our nation.

*"I would suggest that in the area of sexual
indiscretions by public figures we would be
better off adopting a 'don't ask, don't tell'
policy."*

Greater Public Exposure of the Private Lives of Politicians Would Not Benefit America

Patrick McCormick

Patrick McCormick is a professor of ethics at Gonzaga University in Spokane, Washington. In the following viewpoint, he argues that the mass media has spent an inordinate amount of attention on political sex scandals to the exclusion of other important issues. The reason, he surmises, has less to do with informing the public of the importance of character in politics and more to do with attracting audiences and generating profits. While certain sex scandals should be exposed—especially those dealing with sexual harassment, rape, or abuse of power—the private sexual indiscretions of consenting adults should not be the central focus of investigative journalism or public debate, he contends.

As you read, consider the following questions:
1. How is the nation's fixation on President Clinton's sex scandals a reflection of "character," according to McCormick?
2. What distinction does the author make between incidents of sexual abuse and sexual indiscretion?
3. How has Roman Catholic thinking evolved in recent decades concerning the understanding of sin, according to McCormick?

Reprinted with permission from *U.S. Catholic* magazine, Claretian Publications, www.uscatholic.org; 1-800-328-6515, from Patrick McCormick, "When Private Lives Happen to Public People," *U.S. Catholic*, July 1998.

I had a nightmare the other night that Bill Clinton was on the Jerry Springer show. He had been invited there to speak about peace in Northern Ireland and the Middle East, education reform, and his initiative on race, but he found himself sandbagged when Springer revealed that Gennifer Flowers, Paula Jones, Monica Lewinsky, and Kathleen Willey would be joining Clinton for an episode titled "All the President's Women." As a result, Clinton spent the next hour answering accusations and dodging punches thrown by an increasingly hostile audience. There were call-in questions from Ken Starr, Hillary, and Chelsea, and the show ended with a tearfully repentant Clinton accompanying Willie Nelson and Julio Iglesias in a melancholy rendition of "To All the Girls I've Loved Before." It looked like an awful experience for the president. It felt a lot worse to me.

Back in the real world the next morning I noticed at the supermarket checkout counter that Clinton and his entourage were plastered on the covers of all the tabloids; their exploits, accusations, and denials replacing the normal diet of Liz Taylor news, Elvis sightings, and Martian babies. I bought a roll of antacids and a bottle of aspirin. Channel surfing that evening I was pelted by stories about rumored White House imbroglios on *Larry King Live*, *Hard Copy*, *Geraldo Live!*, *Inside Edition*, and *Extra!*

Unfortunately there wasn't much relief on any of the network news shows. In their own ponderous ways Tom Brokaw, Dan Rather, and Peter Jennings were just as obsessed with this "he said-she said" story. I took some more aspirin and went to bed early wishing we still had O.J. to kick around.

Salacious Gossip

Independent Counsel Ken Starr and his backers argue that "we the people" need to care about this story because Clinton's "character" is a matter of political importance. So too the folks in the networks' news rooms seem to believe they are providing a real public service in covering this sordid tale, fulfilling their duties as tough investigative reporters, and defending our constitutional "right" to know what goes on in the various bedrooms (or pantries) of the White House. Where, I wonder, was this free and feisty press during Desert Storm or the invasion of Panama?

Maybe they're right, maybe not, but I suspect that the real truth behind all this concern about Clinton's supposed sexual dalliances is that if there is anything in life more interesting than other people's sex lives, it is the sex lives of celebrities. No matter what Starr and the defenders of a free press argue, the tales of Flowers, Jones, Lewinsky, and Willey (appearing soon, no doubt, in a major motion picture starring Meryl Streep, Sharon Stone, Alicia Silverstone, and Meg Ryan) are getting top billing because they are salacious gossip, and because they sell lots of copy—hard or otherwise.

It's not that we don't need to have public conversations about the character of our leaders and public servants. We certainly do, though perhaps not as much as we need to have sustained conversations about their policies and platforms. (Wasn't it more of a scandal when Candidate Bob Dole argued in 1996 that the contents of the Republican platform really weren't that important?) A well-ordered democracy requires reasonably honorable and competent men and women in the public life—to accept less leads to chaos, to expect more sets us up for demagogues. Character does count.

Junk News

The trouble, however, is that these "public" conversations about character and politics are taking place in the "private" entertainment sector of commercial journalism, where newspapers and networks compete for audience shares and profits by trying to make their product more attractive and "consumer-friendly." As a result, we usually end up reading or talking about whatever publishers or producers think will sell a lot of copies or advertising. And the result, as anyone who has witnessed the tabloidization of the news over the past two decades can tell you, is that it's not just "junk news" shows that are increasingly filled with scandal, gossip, and fluff.

As the major networks and news magazines have been forced into an increasingly competitive market, their stories have gotten shorter, sillier, and sexier. At least in part we're spending more time talking about sex because media owners know that will increase their profits.

So when it's suggested that these tales of sexual scandals are all about character, that may well be true, but they may not be so much about Clinton's character as about the character of our national conversations, our free press, or even our democracy. After all, what would you say about a society spending this much ink and effort on the sexual adventures of its celebrities?

What does it say about us when so much of our public conversation is about the private, confessional concerns of other people? Even more, what are we to make of a White House press corps and political pundits who seem so shocked and angered by the sexual indiscretions of our politicians? Or amazed that someone would lie about such actions? Do Americans really have the puritanical expectation that those elected to public office will be more immune to sexual temptations than the rest of us?

It is one thing to think that such actions are wrong and to hope our public figures won't scandalize us by their behavior. It is quite another to believe these things never take place, that the Clintons really are the Cleavers, or that their sexual troubles are the biggest news in town.

Driven to Distraction

If, as some have argued, these stories are of any real political importance, it is probably because they are displacing other stories we ought and need to be talking about. Every column or report on Monicagate represents a choice to postpone or cancel a conversation about welfare reform, the global environment, or race relations. We like gossip because it's entertaining, but that usually means it's also distracting.

We go to see sexy movies about the presidency like *Wag the Dog*, *Primary Colors*, and *The American President* because we want to escape from the humdrum and difficulties of our day-to-day lives. Fair enough, but that's not supposed to be the function of the evening news.

Part of the problem with all this fascination with sex in the White House is a failure to distinguish between the public and private realms of our lives. Generally, it seems to me, the sexual conduct of people is part of their private lives, and when we forget this and treat the sexual indiscretions or dalliances of our political figures and public servants as if they were concerns of the state it harms us in a couple of ways.

To begin with, if Bill Clinton has no right to privacy, then neither do any of the rest of us, and just how many among us have no personal or family secrets to keep from Larry King or the folks at *60 Minutes*? How many of us could throw that first stone with impunity? Also, allowing chastity to become a character issue in politics could well turn election campaigns into even more puritanical—and hypocritical—mudslinging sideshows, and could scare off lots of valuable talent. Thomas Jefferson and Franklin D. Roosevelt may not have been saints, but both were great presidents.

Walt Handelsman. © Tribune Information Services. All rights reserved. Reprinted with permission.

Since sexual stories are so much juicier and more fascinating than speeches about programs and policies, they can all too easily distract us from the real business of politics, the business of making hard decisions about complex policies that will affect the lives of millions of people. You will always draw a bigger crowd talking about the president's libido than you would addressing environmental or educational issues, but these latter questions are actually the business of state, while the former is water-cooler conversation.

Abuse of Power

Yet this doesn't mean there are no important sexual stories, or that we don't ever need to be concerned about the sexual behavior of our public officials. In the last few years there have been a number of important stories having to do with the sexual conduct or misconduct of political figures and public servants. Tales about sexual harassment or abuse by former Sen. Robert Packwood or former Army Sgt. Maj. Gene McKinney needed to be brought out into the open, thoroughly investigated, and summarily dealt with. Likewise, reports of sexual harassment or rape by drill instructors at Ft. Leonard Wood and Aberdeen, Maryland, as well as the Navy's Tailhook scandal, are a legitimate and urgent public concern.

These cases, involving sexual predators abusing positions of trust, are a matter of public concern for a couple of reasons. First, the right to some privacy in our lives does not entitle us to abuse others with impunity, and we ought not to keep or honor secrets that allow abusers to continue to violate their victims. Blowing the whistle on a predator is the right thing to do.

Second, sexual predators are not engaged in "indiscretions" or "dalliances." Whether it's harassment, rape, or sexual abuse it is not about romance, but about the unjust exercise of power. As such it is fundamentally a political and civil question.

Third, public officials have been granted a position of authority so that they might help the engines of a democratic society run more smoothly. When they violate that trust by abusing their employees, constituents, or those persons entrusted to their care or governance, they are undermining the very nature of public authority. If a senator or soldier has a drinking or gambling problem, if they do not live up to our public standards of personal morality, that is one thing. But if they abuse the very authority needed to make public service effective, it is no longer a private matter. It is a violation of the common good authority is meant to serve.

Follow the Church's Lead

Admittedly the line between cases of indiscretion and abuse is not always crystal clear, and it may well be that we will need to continue to educate ourselves, our press, and our public servants on this distinction. After all, Sen. Packwood seemed to think he was innocent of any real injustice, and clearly some of the furor surrounding the Paula Jones case results from the fact that our understanding of exactly what constitutes harassment is still not firm. Nonetheless, it does seem that we do generally know the difference between sins like adultery and crimes like harassment and rape—even if we continue to need fine-tuning of this knowledge. It also seems that we need to remember this distinction and use it as a guide in making judgments about the relevance of sexual conduct by public officials.

In particular, I would suggest that in the area of sexual indiscretions by public figures we would be better off adopting a "don't ask, don't tell" policy. Such a policy would not keep us (or prosecutors or the press) from looking into charges of harassment, abuse, or rape, but it would prevent us from placing persons like former Air Force Lt. Kelly Flinn or President Clinton in positions where they might feel forced to lie to protect their privacy or good name. It would also keep us from asking possible candidates for the Joint Chiefs of Staff (like former Air Force General Joseph Ralston) about any extramarital affairs they may have had, or reporting on any racy videos Supreme Court justice nominees (like Robert Bork) may have rented at the local video outlet. That is surely information we don't need to have.

One of the great changes in [Roman] Catholic morality after Vatican II [an ecumenical council of the Roman Catholic Church, held from 1962–1965] was a shift in our understanding of sin. Before the council, the great majority of our conversations about sin focused on matters of personal—usually sexual—morality. The old manuals of moral theology paid disproportionate attention to our private sexual lives, as did far too many priests and penitents in the confessional box. Indeed, one 20th-century pontiff even argued that there was no such thing as a "venial" sexual sin. Still, in the past three decades Catholic moral thinking has moved a good distance away from this fixation and given increasing attention to questions of social justice, addressing issues like global poverty, racism, and the dangers of militarization.

Looking at this recent furor about Clinton's sexual affairs, I can't help but believe that we would do well to follow the church's lead in this matter, spending much more of our public debate criticizing our politicians' stance on welfare, education, and the environment, and a lot less talking about the sorts of things we could read about in the tabloids.

"Sadly, we seem more willing to accept leaders who do not exemplify our values."

Voters Should Elect People Who Uphold Their Moral Values

Armstrong Williams

One reason why political scandals occur is that Americans fail to weigh moral issues when electing their political leaders, contends Armstrong Williams in the following viewpoint. Convinced that all politicians are corrupt and that results are all that matter, the public apparently holds the president and other political officials to lower ethical standards than local ministers and teachers. He calls for people to demand of their elected leaders results *and* shared moral values. Williams is a talk show host and syndicated columnist.

As you read, consider the following questions:
1. What do American voters want, according to Williams?
2. Why have voters come to accept lower ethical standards for politicians, according to the author?
3. What does Williams believe Americans should expect from their president?

Reprinted by permission of *The Washington Times* from Armstrong Williams, "Diminished Expectations," *The Washington Times*, October 5, 1996. Copyright 1996 by News World Communications, Inc.

As a nation, we bemoan our decline in morality. Culturally, we watch the entertainment industry produce movies and television programing that undermine the values we want to reinforce in our children. Socially, we continue to grapple with the unfortunate results of government programs meant to assist the poor but which in reality force families apart and trap them in poverty. And politically, we suffer from leaders who aren't able so conduct the nation's business without scandal.

Values and morality are important to us and stir great discussion. Yet, when it comes time to elect political leaders, why don't such issues weigh heavily into our decision?

Can it be that people actually do not care? Have our expectations for our leaders dipped so low that we have discarded morality and values as standards for judgment?

There was a time when we wanted our president to be a leader and role model—but that time has seemingly passed. As scandal after scandal has rocked Washington, as former congressmen face jail time and as political consultants who preach family values fail to practice what they preach, it appears the American people have come to expect less of their leaders. Sadly, we seem more willing to accept leaders who do not exemplify our values.

What Voters Want

Voters today want results. They want inflation low. They want education available. They want their streets safe. They want their military strong. They want their dream of home-ownership alive. They want the future of their children bright.

Voters want a president who can deliver. When [political consultant] James Carville coined the slogan, "It's the economy, stupid!" he knew that people vote their pocketbooks and bank accounts, not their values.

Cynically, many American voters now believe that a candidate's private life is separate from his or her public life. Every day the American media tell us we hold the bar too high—no good people will seek elected office. They tell us if we expect too much, then we will get very little. They tell us we must not hold our leaders to a standard that we our-

selves would not want to be held. They tell us to accept the
flaws—as long as these men and women deliver.

It's all about results. Means justify ends. Our national conscience is being numbed.

Presidents and Teachers

It seems we hold our local ministers and schoolteachers to a
higher standard than we do our president. Think about it. If
our minister or a schoolteacher was perpetually surrounded
by scandal, we would seek that person's removal. We would
not ask questions about his or her performance, even though
that performance might be exemplary. We would not ask,
"But how does he preach?" or "But does she prepare good
lessons?" We would not ignore the private life for the sake
of professional performance. Instead, we would hold such
people to the highest possible standard and dismiss them; we
want not just people who get results but people *with values*
who get results.

Why then do we seem satisfied with a president who just
gets results rather than seeking a president who exemplifies
our values and gets results?

Maybe people no longer believe they can have both. Maybe people have been so beaten down by immorality and the "dog-eat-dog" nature of the world that they have given up hope. Maybe people have grown so tired from the daily struggles and so conscious of their own human flaws that they just don't expect much from their leaders.

Every day you hear people comment, "Well, they are all just corrupt anyway." I used to think that was just something people say. But I was wrong—people actually mean it. More and more people believe that everyone willing to run for office must be corrupt in some way. Therefore, they are willing to accept moral and ethical flaws in candidates that they would never accept in anyone else.

What a terrible way to select a national leader!

We should not settle for a president who just gets results. We should demand a president who gets results and shares our values as well. America deserves an honorable president.

| *"A political leader who is morally reckless at home may or may not be reckless in office."*

Voters Should Not Use Private Moral Values as a Guide to Electing Officials

Michael Walzer

Michael Walzer is an author and contributing editor to the *New Republic*; his books include *Spheres of Justice: A Defense of Pluralism and Equality*. In the following viewpoint, he argues that people's behavior in their private lives has little bearing on what kind of public official they would be. He argues that voters in a constitutional democracy such as the United States should, rather than focus on their private character, instead select candidates that uphold certain political values such as faith to the Constitution, commitment to democracy, and trustworthiness. Politicians who fail to live up to these standards should be dealt with by voting them out of office.

As you read, consider the following questions:

1. What 1960s slogan does Walzer question?
2. What three values does Walzer say are important in public life?
3. What distinction does the author make between a monarchy and a constitutional democracy in terms of the behavior of its leaders?

From Michael Walzer, "Getting Personal," *The New Republic*, March 16, 1998. Copyright 1998 by The New Republic, Inc. Reprinted by permission of *The New Republic*.

Even in the '60s, I was uneasy with the slogan "the personal is political." There was a sense in which it was important and true. It suggested that the inequalities of everyday life, above all, the gender inequalities, should not be understood as "merely" private, for that is the false understanding that entrenches and perpetuates them. In fact, they are socially patterned; they are often recognized in the law, reinforced by bureaucratic procedures; and therefore in need of political opposition and reform.

But the slogan was also taken to mean that the everyday behavior of men and women in their private lives is closely connected to, or at least indicative of, their likely behavior in public life. And that proposition is almost certainly false. It would be nice if it were true: if marital faithfulness, parental concern, true friendship, fidelity to campaign promises, loyalty to the cause, compassion, political courage, moral vision, and moral authority all went together, so that if candidate X, say, is faithful to his friends and relatives, we could be sure that he will be faithful to the party program; if he is faithful to the program, his friends and relatives have nothing to worry about. Conservative writers often use the word "character" to describe what supposedly underlies the qualities on my list. Find men and women with character, and you can count on them, in public and private, good times and bad; they will always act in the morally right way. Sometimes the argument goes one step further: they won't only be good, they will also be good at all the things that they need to do.

Unfortunately, these claims aren't true, and we all know that they aren't true. We all know, or we have heard about, people who represent every possible combination of good and bad qualities—mass murderers who are loving husbands and fathers; thieves and philanderers who are decent, competent, even inspiring political leaders. There is no formula for sorting all this out. Democratic citizens use their common sense. . . .

Political Morality

Still, it is worth thinking about what a political morality might look like. What are the standards by which we should measure our leaders and representatives? I have a short list,

71

designed to suggest the counter-slogan: the political isn't personal. Maybe the list is too short. But it seems to me that most of what we ought to want, and deserve to have, in our public officials is encompassed by three values:

John Trever for the *Albuquerque Journal*. Reprinted with permission.

Constitutional faith. When they come into office, political leaders take an oath to the Constitution, and thereby accept a set of obligations, which are probably best stated in negative terms: no tampering with the democratic process; no effort to undermine the separation of powers; no denial of the guaranteed rights of citizens, including, most importantly, the right of opposition. This is the realm where violations of trust are most dangerous, and I am inclined to think that the independent counsel law ought to be focused here. Only when there is serious evidence of constitutional crimes is there sufficient reason for a special prosecutor, who is set radically free from any pressure that could be brought to bear by the people who may have committed the crimes. But crimes of passion, enrichment, and even violence (unless the violence is directed at political enemies) should probably be handled by the normal justice system. If normal justice can't do the job, it should be strengthened, not displaced.

Democratic commitment. Public officials ought to be committed all the time to all the citizens. They have to think about the common good even when they are acting in inevitably particularist ways. When they do cost-benefit analysis, they have to count everyone's costs and benefits, without regard to class, race, or religion. Of course, even the narrowest partisanship isn't usually a matter for criminal investigation. Political leaders who serve the rich and the powerful, for example, have only sometimes been paid for their services. But they are morally culpable even when the service is selfless, for they ought to address themselves to the needs of the poor and the weak. This requirement has to be politically enforced, say, through elections, despite the fact that political enforcement is always partial and belated. I confess that I might enjoy the spectacle of a special prosecutor collecting the private papers, or taping the phone conversations, of political leaders who are suspected of never thinking about fellow citizens in trouble. But that kind of righteous zeal leads only to tyranny. (It wouldn't be so bad, though, if energetic journalists pursued such matters, without legal powers or invasive technology.)

Trustworthiness. I mean here to describe (only!) political honesty: good-faith relationships with constituents, party members, colleagues, and subordinates in the government itself. It is true that in democratic political campaigns the promises of candidates are always discounted; we don't in fact expect exactly what we are told to expect. But we ought to insist on a general programmatic commitment, and, when officeholders break that commitment, we ought to require a public accounting. Here again, there is no room for litigation. Political promises are not contracts, and they can only be enforced politically.

This is even more obviously true with regard to the promises exchanged among politicians when they agree to support a particular piece of legislation or to join some policy coalition. Trust is crucial in these kinds of relationships. It would not be a good thing if all politicians were wired with hidden microphones while negotiating with their colleagues. When trust breaks down, we all pay a price, because leaders who can't be trusted will not be able to do things that ought to be done: to take necessary risks or to ask for sacrifices from their own supporters or from the nation as a whole. Trust is a kind of political capital that has to be accumulated over long periods of time, in preparation for those critical moments when it must be suddenly spent.

Excluding Private Lives

By limiting the list this way, excluding the private lives of political leaders, I don't mean to deny that common decency and personal integrity figure importantly in public life. But I don't know exactly how they figure, and I am not eager to speculate. A political leader who is morally reckless at home may or may not be reckless in office. He may, in fact, be excessively circumspect and cautious. The contrast between democracy and monarchy is instructive here: the private recklessness of kings and queens threatens the legitimacy of the dynasty and the peacefulness of the succession. Not so for us. We can and should judge politicians by what they do politically. We need to know as much as we can about their vision for the country and about their competence in achieving that vision and about their readiness to restrain their efforts within the limits of a constitutional democracy. For myself, I don't think that I want to know anything more.

Periodical Bibliography

The following articles have been selected to supplement the diverse views presented in this chapter. Addresses are provided for periodicals not indexed in the *Readers' Guide to Periodical Literature*, the *Alternative Press Index*, the *Social Sciences Index*, or the *Index to Legal Periodicals and Books*.

Russell Baker — "Fire, Ice, and Farce," *New York Times*, October 9, 1998.

Peter Beinart — "Private Matters: How the Personal Became Political," *New Republic*, February 15, 1999.

Ken Bode — "To Tell the Truth," *New Republic*, September 13–20, 1999.

William F. Buckley — "Did You Ever Commit Adultery?" *National Review*, February 8, 1999.

Jean Bethke Elshtain — "Beyond Consent," *New Republic*, May 4, 1998.

Lynda Hurst — "History Repeats Itself—Again," *World Press Review*, April 1998.

John F. Kavanaugh — "Sex, Lies, and Politics," *America*, August 29–September 5, 1998.

David Kirby — "Sexual McCarthyism," *Advocate*, February 2, 1999.

Richard Lacayo — "Cover That Keyhole," *Time*, October 5, 1998.

William Safire — "Sin Is Private and Crime Is Public," *Conservative Chronicle*, February 4, 1998. Available from Box 29, Hampton, IA 50441.

Richard Shenkman — "Sex, Lies, and Presidents," *Washington Monthly*, October 1998.

Janna Malamud Smith — "The Adultery Wars," *New York Times*, December 19, 1998.

John F. Stacks — "Is Nothing Private?" *Time*, August 23, 1999.

Andrew Sullivan — "Not a Straight Story," *New York Times Magazine*, December 12, 1999.

Cynthia Tucker — "Private Behavior Is Not Always a Gauge of Public Conduct," *Liberal Opinion*, February 2, 1998. Available from PO Box 880, Vinton, IA 52349.

James M. Wall — "True Compassion," *Christian Century*, September 8–15, 1999.

Anthony Wilson-Smith — "Private Lives, Public People," *Maclean's*, September 6, 1999.

CHAPTER 3

Case Study: Was President Bill Clinton's Impeachment Justified?

Chapter Preface

The U.S. Constitution provides for impeachment and removal from office of the president, vice president, and other government officials for "Conviction of Treason, Bribery, or Other High Crimes and Misdemeanors." Under the Constitution, the House of Representatives has the sole power of impeachment—the bringing of formal charges against the president or other official. The Senate then holds a trial on the House's accusations (with the Chief Justice of the Supreme Court presiding), with a two-thirds vote necessary for conviction and removal from office.

Impeachment has been referred to as the "atomic bomb" of the American system of government—a necessary tool to combat scandalous and tyrannical actions of the nation's leaders, but one that should not be used lightly. Only fifteen impeachment trails have taken place in the Senate, most involving federal judges. In all of American history, only three presidents have faced impeachment. In 1868 Andrew Johnson, who had serious policy differences with Congress, was impeached by the House of Representatives in 1868 on counts of usurping legislative authority and removing executive branch officers without Congress's approval. After a trial in the Senate, he was acquitted by one vote. In 1974, following the Watergate scandal, the House Judiciary committee approved three articles of impeachment against Richard Nixon for abuses of executive power including illegal wiretapping and misuses of the Central Intelligence Agency (CIA). Nixon saved himself from almost certain impeachment by resigning. Finally, in 1998, Bill Clinton was impeached for perjury and obstruction of justice for allegedly attempting to cover up a sexual affair with a former White House intern, Monica Lewinsky.

Much of the evidence against Clinton was gathered and reported to Congress by independent counsel Kenneth W. Starr. In 1994, under a statute inspired by Nixon's resignation under scandal, Starr was appointed to investigate certain real estate transactions Clinton made while governor of Arkansas (the Whitewater scandal). Starr's office was subsequently authorized by Attorney General Janet Reno to investigate other allegedly scandalous activities surrounding the Clinton administration, including the president's relationship with Lewinsky. In a separate sexual harassment case deposition on January 17, 1998, Clinton denied under oath his relationship with Lewinsky and repeated his denial for months after the story became public on January 21. In his September 9, 1998, report to Congress, Starr said nothing about Whitewater, but concluded that Clinton had committed perjury regarding his relationship with Lewinsky and had obstructed justice in the sexual harassment case by seeking to buy Lewinsky's complicity with a job offer. Clinton then admitted to an "improper" relationship with Lewinsky, but refused to resign.

On December 19, 1998, Bill Clinton became the second president in U.S. history to be impeached. The House of Representatives voted to impeach him on two articles of perjury and obstruction of justice. On February 12, 1999, following a thirty-seven-day trail, the Senate voted to acquit the president of the two articles of impeachment; neither article attained majority support, let alone the two-thirds necessary for conviction. Disagreement and controversy continues to surround the questions of how impeachment will affect Clinton's historical legacy and whether such a trial should have been allowed to go forward. The viewpoints in this chapter examine these questions.

> "[President Clinton] has disgraced himself
> and the high office he holds. His high
> crimes and misdemeanors undermine our
> Constitution."

President Clinton Has Committed Impeachable Offenses

House Judiciary Committee

On December 11 and 12, 1998, following a series of hearings, the House Judiciary Committee approved four articles of impeachment against President Bill Clinton. The vote was on party lines, with Republicans favoring and Democrats opposing impeachment. In the following viewpoint, taken from the official statement of the committee, the members who supported impeachment argue why they had taken this step. They accuse Clinton of perjury and obstruction of justice in failing to be fully candid about a sexual affair, and maintain that he thereby failed to uphold his presidential oath to "preserve, protect, and defend the Constitution of the United States." On December 19, 1998, the full House of Representatives, again voting mostly on party lines, approved two of the four impeachment articles.

As you read, consider the following questions:

1. What important principle of the U.S. government is the committee attempting to uphold, according to its report?
2. How did President Bill Clinton violate his oath of office to preserve the Constitution, according to the committee?

Reprinted from "The Case Against President Clinton," *Congressional Digest*, February 1999, originally from the House Judiciary Committee Report 105-830, *The Impeachment of William Jefferson Clinton, President of the United States*, December 15, 1998.

E qual Justice Under Law. That principle so embodies the American constitutional order that we have carved it in stone on the front of our Supreme Court. The carving shines like a beacon from the highest sanctum of the Judicial Branch across to the Capitol, the home of the Legislative Branch, and down Pennsylvania Avenue to the White House, the home of the Executive Branch. It illuminates our national life and reminds those other branches that despite the tumbling tides of politics, ours is a government of laws and not of men. It was the inspired vision of our Founders and Framers that the Judicial, Legislative, and Executive Branches would work together to preserve the rule of law.

Consequences for Average Citizens

But "Equal Justice Under Law" amounts to much more than a stone carving. Although we cannot see or hear it, this living breathing force has real consequences in the lives of average citizens every day. Ultimately, it protects us from the knock on the door in the middle of the night. More commonly, it allows us to claim the assistance of the government when someone has wronged us—even if that person is stronger or wealthier or more popular than we are. In America, unlike other countries, when the average citizen sues the Chief Executive of our Nation, they stand equal before the bar of justice. The Constitution requires the Judicial Branch of our government to apply the law equally to both. That is the living consequence of "Equal Justice Under Law."

The President of the United States must work with the Judicial and Legislative Branches to sustain that force. The temporary trustee of that office, William Jefferson Clinton, worked to defeat it. When he stood before the bar of justice, he acted without authority to award himself the special privileges of lying and obstructing to gain an advantage in a Federal civil rights action in the U.S. District Court for the Eastern District of Arkansas, in a Federal grand jury investigation in the U.S. District Court for the District of Columbia, and in an impeachment inquiry in the U.S. House of Representatives. His resistance brings us to this most unfortunate juncture.

So "Equal Justice Under Law" lies at the heart of this

matter. It rests on three essential pillars: an impartial judiciary, an ethical bar, and a sacred oath. If litigants profane the sanctity of the oath, "Equal Justice Under Law" loses its protective force. Against that backdrop, consider the actions of President Clinton.

Article I of President Clinton's Impeachment

In his conduct while President of the United States, William Jefferson Clinton, in violation of his constitutional oath faithfully to execute the office of President of the United States and, to the best of his ability, preserve, protect, and defend the Constitution of the United States, and in violation of his constitutional duty to take care that the laws be faithfully executed, has willfully corrupted and manipulated the judicial process of the United States for his personal gain and exoneration, impeding the administration of justice, in that:

On August 17, 1998, William Jefferson Clinton swore to tell the truth, the whole truth, and nothing but the truth before a Federal grand jury of the United States. Contrary to that oath, William Jefferson Clinton willfully provided perjurious, false, and misleading testimony to the grand jury concerning one or more of the following: (1) the nature and details of his relationship with a subordinate government employee; (2) prior perjurious, false, and misleading testimony he gave in a Federal civil rights action brought against him; (3) prior false and misleading statements he allowed his attorney to make to a Federal judge in that civil rights action; and (4) his corrupt efforts to influence the testimony of witnesses and to impede the discovery of evidence in that civil rights action. In doing this, William Jefferson Clinton has undermined the integrity of his office, has brought disrepute on the Presidency, has betrayed his trust as President, and has acted in a manner subversive of the rule of law and justice, to the manifest injury of the people of the United States.

Congressional Digest, February 1999.

On May 27, 1997, the nine justices of the Supreme Court of the United States unanimously ruled that Paula Corbin Jones could pursue her Federal civil rights actions against William Jefferson Clinton. On December 11, 1997, U.S. District Judge Susan Webber Wright ordered President Clinton to provide Ms. Jones with answers to certain routine questions relevant to the [sexual harassment] lawsuit. Acting under the authority of these court orders, Ms. Jones exercised her rights—rights that every litigant has under our system of justice. She sought answers from President Clinton to help her prove her case against him—just as President Clinton sought and received answers from her. President Clinton used numerous means to prevent her from getting truthful answers.

On December 17, 1997, he encouraged a witness [Monica Lewinsky], whose truthful testimony would have helped Ms. Jones, to file a false affidavit in the case and to testify falsely if she were called to testify in the case. On December 23, 1997, he provided, under oath, false written answers to Ms. Jones's questions. On December 28, 1997, he began an effort to get the witness to conceal evidence that would have helped Ms. Jones. Throughout this period, he intensified efforts to provide the witness with help in getting a job to ensure that she carried out his designs.

On January 17, 1998, President Clinton provided, under oath, numerous false answers to Ms. Jones's questions during his deposition. In the days immediately following the deposition, he provided a false and misleading account to another witness, Betty Currie, in hopes that she would substantiate the false testimony he gave in the deposition. These actions denied Ms. Jones her rights as a litigant, subverted the fundamental truth-seeking function of the U.S. District Court for the Eastern District of Arkansas, and violated President Clinton's constitutional oath to "preserve, protect, and defend the Constitution of the United States" and his constitutional duty to "take care that the laws be faithfully executed."

Beginning shortly after his deposition, President Clinton became aware that a Federal grand jury empaneled by the U.S. District Court for the District of Columbia was investigating his actions before and during his civil deposition. President Clinton made numerous false statements to potential grand jury witnesses in hopes that they would repeat these statements to the grand jury. On August 17, 1998, President Clinton appeared before the grand jury by video and, under oath, provided numerous false answers to the questions asked. These actions impeded the grand jury's investigation, subverted the fundamental truth-seeking function of the U.S. District Court for the District of Columbia, and violated President Clinton's constitutional oath to "preserve, protect, and defend the Constitution of the United States" and his constitutional duty to "take care that the laws be faithfully executed."

President Clinton's actions then led to this inquiry. On October 8, 1998, the U.S. House of Representatives passed H.Res. 581, directing the Committee on the judiciary to begin an inquiry to determine whether President Clinton should be impeached. As part of that inquiry, the Committee sent written requests for admissions to him. On November 27, 1998, President Clinton provided, under oath, numerous false statements to this committee in response to the requests for admission. These actions impeded the committee's inquiry, subverted the fundamental truth-seeking function of the U.S. House of Representatives in exercising the sole power of impeachment, and violated President Clinton's constitutional oath to "preserve, protect, and defend the Constitution of the United States" and his constitutional duty to "take care that the laws be faithfully executed."

High Crimes and Misdemeanors

By these actions, President Clinton violated the sanctity of the oath without which "Equal Justice Under Law" cannot survive. Rather than work with the Judicial and Legislative Branches to uphold the rule of law, he directly attacked their fundamental truth-seeking function. He has disgraced himself and the high office he holds. His high crimes and misdemeanors undermine our Constitution. They warrant his impeachment, his removal from office, and his disqualification from holding further office.

"There is far from sufficient evidence to support the allegations, and the allegations, even if proven, do not rise to the level of impeachable offenses."

President Clinton Has Not Committed Impeachable Offenses

Jerrold Nadler

Jerrold Nadler is a U.S. Representative from New York. He was one of the fifteen democrats on the House Judiciary Committee to vote against articles of impeachment against President Bill Clinton that the committee adopted in December 1998. In the following viewpoint, taken from his December 19, 1998, statement before the full House of Representatives, Nadler argues that not enough evidence supports the accusations of perjury and obstruction of justice brought against Clinton by independent counsel Kenneth Starr. In addition, he argues that the impeachment process is meant to remove officials whose actions seriously threaten the U.S. government. Nadler maintains that Clinton's alleged offenses stemming from the attempted concealment of a private sexual affair do not meet this criterion.

As you read, consider the following questions:
1. Why, in Nadler's opinion, might perjury not be an impeachable offense?
2. What conclusions have the American people made about President Bill Clinton, according to the author?
3. What questions does Nadler raise about the evidence gathered against Clinton?

Excerpted from Jerrold Nadler's arguments during the House of Representatives floor debate of December 19, 1998, concerning impeachment of President Clinton, as reprinted in the *Congressional Digest*, February 1999.

For only the second time in our Nation's history, this House meets to consider articles of impeachment against a President of the United States. This is a momentous occasion, and I would hope that, despite the sharp partisan tone which has marked this debate, we can approach it with a sober sense of the historic importance of this matter.

The history of the language is also clear. At the Constitutional Convention, the Committee on Style, which was not authorized to make any substantive changes, dropped the words "against the United States" after the words "high crimes and misdemeanors" because it was understood that only high crimes and misdemeanors against the system of government would be impeachable—that the words "against the United States" were redundant and unnecessary.

History and the precedents alike show that impeachment is not a punishment for crimes but a means to protect the constitutional system, and it was certainly not meant to be a means to punish a President for personal wrongdoing not related to his office. Some of our Republican colleagues have made much of the fact that some of the Democrats on this committee in 1974 voted in favor of an article of impeachment relating to President Nixon's alleged perjury on his tax returns, but the plain fact is that a bipartisan vote of that Committee—something we have not yet had in this process on any substantive question—rejected that article.

That's the historical record, and it was largely based on the belief that an impeachable offense must be an abuse of Presidential power, a "great and dangerous offense against the Nation," not perjury on a private matter.

We are told that perjury is as serious an offense as bribery, a per se impeachable offense. But bribery goes to the heart of the President's conduct of his constitutional duties. It converts his loyalties and efforts from promoting the welfare of the Republic to promoting some other interest.

Perjury is a serious crime—and, if provable, should be prosecuted in a court of law. But it may, or may not, involve the President's duties and performance in office. Perjury on a private matter—perjury regarding sex—is not a "great and dangerous offense against the Nation." It is not an abuse of uniquely Presidential power. It does not threaten our form of government. It is not an impeachable offense.

The effect of impeachment is to overturn the popular will of the voters as expressed in a national election. We must not overturn an election and remove a President from office except to defend our very system of government and our constitutional liberties against a dire threat. And we must not do so without an overwhelming consensus of the American people and of their Representatives in Congress on its absolute necessity.

There must never be a narrowly voted impeachment, or an impeachment substantially supported by one of our major political parties and largely opposed by the other. Such an impeachment will lack legitimacy, will produce divisiveness and bitterness in our politics for years to come, and will call into question the legitimacy of our political institutions.

The American people have heard all the allegations against the President and they overwhelmingly oppose impeaching him. The people elected President Clinton. They still support him. We have no right to overturn the considered judgment of the American people. . . .

A Weak Case

Mr. [Kenneth] Starr has stated in his referral to Congress that his own "star witness" [Monica Lewinsky] is not credible, except when her uncorroborated testimony conflicts with the President's, and then it proves his perjury.

We have received sanctimonious lectures from the other side about the "rule of law," but the law does not permit perjury to be proved by the uncorroborated testimony of one witness. Nor does the law recognize as corroboration the fact that the witness made the same statement to several different people. You may choose to believe that the President was disingenuous, that he was not particularly helpful to Paula Jones' lawyers when they asked him intentionally vague questions, or that he is a bum, but that does not make him guilty of perjury.

This House is not a grand jury. To impeach the President would subject the country to the trauma of a trial in the Senate. It would paralyze the government for many months while the problems of Social Security, Medicare, a deteriorating world economy, and all our foreign concerns festered without proper attention.

We cannot simply punt the duty to judge the facts to the Senate if we find mere "probable cause" that an impeachable offense may have been committed. To do so would be a derogation of our constitutional duty. The proponents of impeachment have provided no direct evidence of impeachable offenses. They rely solely on the findings of an "independent" counsel [Starr] who has repeatedly mischaracterized evidence, failed to include exculpatory evidence, and consistently misstated the law.

High Crimes?

The Constitution calls for impeachment for "treason, bribery or other high crimes and misdemeanors." The "other" suggests that those crimes be on the order of treason and bribery. Is Clinton's lying about whether he touched Monica Lewinsky's breasts comparable to treason? Is Clinton's lying about whether he thought oral sex was sex comparable to bribery? . . .

Republicans say that any lying under oath—even if in response to sexual questions that few Americans would answer—is a high crime because it undermines the rule of law, the foundation of our democratic stability. But which does more damage to that stability—leaving a lying president (hardly the first) in office, or having a full-blown constitutional crisis over his removal?

Jonathan Alter, *Newsweek*, December 21, 1998.

We must not be a rubber stamp for Kenneth Starr. We have been entrusted with this grave and dangerous duty by the American people, by the Constitution, and by history. We must exercise that duty responsibly.

At a bare minimum, that means the President's accusers must go beyond hearsay and innuendo, and beyond demands that the President prove his innocence of vague and changing charges. They must provide clear and convincing evidence of specific impeachable conduct. This they have failed to do.

If you believe the President's admission to the grand jury and to the Nation of an inappropriate sexual relationship with Ms. Lewinsky, and his apologies to the Nation, were not abject enough, that is not a reason for impeachment. Contrition is a remedy for sin, and is certainly appropriate here. But while insufficiency of contrition may leave the soul still scarred, unexpiated sin proves no crimes and justifies no impeachment.

Is the President Above the Law?

Some say that if we do not impeach the President, we treat him as if he is above the law.

Is the President above the law? Certainly not. He is subject to the criminal law—to indictment and prosecution when he leaves office—like any other citizen, whether or not he is impeached. And if the Republican leadership allows a vote, he would likely be the third President in U.S. history, and the first since 1848, to be censured by the Congress.

But impeachment is intended as a remedy to protect the Nation, not as a punishment for a President.

The case is not there. There is far from sufficient evidence to support the allegations, and the allegations, even if proven, do not rise to the level of impeachable offenses. We should not dignify these articles of impeachment by sending them to the Senate. To do so would be an affront to the Constitution and would consign this House to the condemnation of history for generations to come.

"Clearly, nothing Clinton did sinks to the depths of what Nixon did."

The Lewinsky Scandal Is Not Comparable to Watergate

Eric Pooley

In September 1998 Kenneth Starr, a special prosecutor who had been investigating several potential scandals surrounding President Bill Clinton, delivered a report to Congress. In the report, which Congress soon made public, Starr concluded that Clinton had committed impeachable offenses over the course of concealing an affair with an intern, Monica Lewinsky. In the following viewpoint, *Time* magazine writer Eric Pooley reports on the findings of the Starr report and compares Clinton's actions to the Watergate scandal that resulted in President Richard Nixon's 1974 resignation under threat of impeachment. Nixon, Pooley argues, misused his presidential authority to harass his political enemies, then sought to cover up his questionable actions and those of his subordinates. Clinton's lies and obstructions, Pooley concludes, were at bottom the result of an attempt to hide from the public a sordid sexual affair and are not really comparable to Nixon's situation.

As you read, consider the following questions:

1. What role did President Clinton have in creating Lewinsky's affidavit denying a sexual relationship, according to the author?
2. Why did Clinton and many Americans believe Starr's investigation into the Lewinsky affair to be lacking in legitimacy, according to the author?

I feel like a character in a novel," Bill Clinton told an aide on the day the Lewinsky scandal broke. With equal parts self-pity and deceit, the President cast himself as the protagonist in *Darkness at Noon*, Arthur Koestler's 1941 classic about the victim of a totalitarian witch-hunt. Eight months later, in the pages of Kenneth Starr's report to Congress, Clinton finds himself the villain in a much trashier tale, a fetid blend of libido and legalese that reads like Jackie Collins by way of the *Congressional Quarterly*. . . .

As numbing and repetitive as any porn, the narrative is clinical and sad, a recitation of furtive gropings and panicky zipping-ups between two profoundly needy people, one of whom happened to be the leader of the free world. While Clinton's lawyers thunder that the endless tawdry details serve no purpose but to "humiliate the President and force him from office," Starr argues that Clinton himself made them necessary. Starr's office had originally planned to confine the seamier material to a secret sex appendix, a Starr ally told *Time*. But because the President lied so long and hard, the report maintains, Starr had no choice but to include the particulars that proved that . . . Clinton and Lewinsky had sex, and Clinton lied to cover it up.

No one outside the White House will be quibbling there, thanks to Lewinsky's phenomenal memory and careful record keeping. Awestruck and infatuated though she may have been, Lewinsky was a cool and precise recorder of every moment she spent with Clinton—what they said and did, which Secret Service agents were warily watching them come and go, which aides were shooting daggers at her outside the Oval Office, which phone calls Clinton took during their time together. The narrative relies on Lewinsky's testimony for the particulars of 10 alleged sexual encounters, but to bolster her credibility—she did, after all, perjure herself in her Jones affidavit and cooperated with Starr in exchange for immunity—the report time and again uses White House records and contemporaneous accounts to corroborate her stories. Lewinsky remembers being with Clinton on President's Day 1996, when he spoke to a Florida sugar grower named "something like Fanuli." Phone logs show Clinton spoke to sugar baron Alfonso Fanjul that day. Lewinsky says that during three sexual encounters, Clinton was on the phone with Congressmen; during another, he took a call from his disgraced consultant Dick Morris; in each case, phone logs bear out her account. . . .

The relationship was facilitated by Betty Currie, Clinton's private secretary, a motherly, church going woman who acted as go-between: setting up meetings for Clinton and Lewinsky, connecting them by telephone but not always logging the calls, passing Lewinsky's letters and parcels to him unopened, finding ways to get her into the White House past hostile presidential aides and even coming to the White House on weekends just to escort Lewinsky to the President. Currie had her suspicions, at the very least, but tried hard to stay in the dark. Lewinsky once told her that if no one saw Monica and Clinton together, then nothing had happened. "Don't want to hear it," Currie replied, according to Lewinsky. "Don't say any more. I don't want to hear any more."

Currie was the perfect assistant to a man who had been concealing sex for decades. Starr alleges no fewer than five Clinton perjuries in the [January 17, 1998, Paula] Jones deposition on the issue of whether the President and Lewinsky had a sexual affair, three more in Clinton's Aug. 17 [1998] grand-jury testimony (claiming, for example, that he hadn't touched Lewinsky's breasts or genitals) and one lie in his televised statement to the American people that night, when he said his Jones testimony had been "legally accurate." The President, Starr also alleges, lied when he claimed he couldn't recall being alone with Lewinsky, lied when he said he hadn't discussed her Jones affidavit with her, lied when he said he hadn't helped her find a job. Since perjury is exceptionally difficult to prove—especially when the witness is as skilled at evasion as Clinton—it is questionable whether any of these misleading statements could be grounds for impeachment, as the prosecutor claims. And there is reason to recoil at some of Starr's tactics; he included far more sexual detail than was necessary to prove his point, and at times ignored or discounted evidence that contradicts his case. Still, many Americans—even those who have long assumed Clinton was lying—will be appalled by the depths of the President's recklessness and deceit. Others will say, Tell us something we didn't know.

So Starr tells them. After the initial shock wears off, readers may find the most damaging sections of the report to be not the salacious details that demonstrate Clinton's deceit but rather the staggeringly detailed account of the cover-up effort he directed: a campaign to avoid discovery that, Starr alleges, amounts to abusing the powers of the office to stymie Starr's investigation. Though the outlines of the story have long since been told in press accounts, the report offers scores of damning new details that drive home the truth of a 25-year-old cliche: the cover-up is worse than the crime.

Comparing Watergate and Clinton

Watergate was about a vast and pervasive abuse of power and authority by a criminal president of the United States. President Nixon ordered break-ins and fire-bombings. He hired a goon squad to thwart the electoral process. He used the agencies of government to harass his political opponents and ordered illegal wiretaps of reporters and of his own aides. Literally, he authorized the mechanisms of a police state. And he presided over a cover-up in which hundreds of thousands of dollars were paid to keep the Watergate burglars quiet.

The Clinton case is not about this kind of abuse of presidential authority. From the available facts, this would appear to be a sex scandal in which the president apparently lied under oath in a civil case and may have even obstructed justice in an attempt to hide a truly reckless consensual relationship with a White House intern almost as young as his daughter.

So this is a far cry from Watergate. At the same time, when the president of the United States lies under oath, it is serious business.

Carl Bernstein, *New Perspectives Quarterly*, Fall 1998.

Most accounts have dated Clinton's alleged scheme to buy Lewinsky's silence by finding her a New York job to the fall of 1997, when she was named as a possible witness in the Jones suit. But the report demonstrates that its roots went back much further. By early spring of that year, according to the report, Clinton began focusing on the threat Lewinsky represented, asking her whether she had told her mother, Marcia Lewis, of the affair. Word of the relationship had leaked to Lewis' friend, Walter Kaye, who mentioned it to

White House aide Marsha Scott. Not long after that, Lewinsky received an invitation from Betty Currie to visit the President. On Saturday, May 24, Clinton told Lewinsky he wanted to break off the affair. The President noted, she testified, that "he could do a great deal for her."

Three days later, the Supreme Court ruled that the Jones case could proceed during Clinton's term. Soon after that decision, Jones' lawyers announced they would try to find other female subordinates who had been approached sexually by Clinton. That gave him an even stronger motive for helping Lewinsky. The report details a truly extraordinary job search on her behalf, one driven in part by Lewinsky's extortionate demands. . . .

By autumn [of 1997], the stakes were rising for Clinton. On Oct. 1, he received interrogatories from Jones' lawyers asking for a list of women other than his wife with whom he had sought to have sexual relations. Six days later, Lewinsky sent the President another letter complaining about her stalled job search. . . . After 2 a.m. on Oct. 10, the report says, Clinton called Lewinsky and unloaded on her: "If I had known what kind of person you really were, I never would have gotten involved with you," he told her. She complained that he had not done enough to help her. Clinton said he was eager to help. She told him she wanted a job in New York City by the end of October, and he promised to try.

The next day, a Saturday, she was invited for a visit with Clinton, according to the report. They met in the study and discussed jobs. He told her to prepare a list of New York companies she wanted to work for. She suggested that the hyperconnected lawyer Vernon Jordan might help. Clinton was receptive. . . .

It fell to Jordan to find the right job. In his testimony, he claimed to have received assurances from Lewinsky and Clinton that there was no sex. But Lewinsky testified that Jordan knew "with a wink and a nod that I was having a relationship with the President." Just after the Oct. 11 meeting in which Monica suggested to Clinton that Jordan help her find a job, Clinton spoke to him by phone. Clinton has testified that it was Currie who brought Jordan into the effort. But Lewinsky testified that Currie called Jordan at the

President's initiative. Jordan, who met Lewinsky in November, said he assumed the same.

Jordan moved slowly at first; he had no contact with Lewinsky for more than a month. But by Dec. 6, Clinton had even more reason to placate the woman: his lawyers showed him a list of witnesses the Jones team was planning to call. Among them was Lewinsky. On Sunday, Dec. 7, Jordan met with the President at the White House. Jordan denied that Lewinsky or the Jones case was discussed, but four days later he was meeting with Lewinsky for the second time, giving her the names of three business contacts. Later that day he called three executives to recommend her. . . .

The President was now devoting a lot of attention to the Monica problem. After 2 a.m. on Dec. 17, he called her at home and told her she was on the witness list. According to Lewinsky, he told her that "it broke his heart" to see her listed. But if she were subpoenaed, he said, "she could sign an affidavit to try to satisfy the inquiry and not be deposed." He also went over what Lewinsky calls one of the "cover stories" they had discussed as the affair unfolded: her frequent visits to the White House were to see her friend Currie. Starr calls this a case of subornation of perjury. Clinton testified that he didn't recall saying it.

Over the next couple of days, the twin worries of affidavit and job only grew. So did Jordan's role. On Dec. 18 and 23, Lewinsky interviewed at two New York firms contacted by Jordan. On Dec. 19, she was served with a subpoena to testify in the Jones case. On Dec. 22, Jordan took Lewinsky to her new attorney, and the two discussed her job prospects, the subpoena and the Jones case during the ride in his limousine. . . .

The report suggests an active role by Clinton in creating Lewinsky's affidavit denying a sexual relationship. He had suggested the affidavit in the first place, and though Lewinsky says he never explicitly asked her to lie, they had often discussed keeping their relationship secret. As Lewinsky told Linda Tripp in a recorded conversation, "I don't think he thinks of [it as] lying under oath. . . . He thinks of it as . . . 'We're being smart; we're being safe; it's good for everybody.'" Jordan testified that Clinton was "concerned about the affidavit and whether it was signed or not," and he had kept up "a continuing dialogue" with Clinton on the matter. Phone records for Jan. 6 [1998], for example, show Jordan in contact with the White House twice, Lewinsky three times and her attorney Carter four times. In one flurry, Jordan called the President less than 30 minutes after speaking with Lewinsky and then called Carter immediately after that.

On Jan. 7, Lewinsky signed the affidavit and brought a copy to show Jordan. He placed three long calls to the White House that day in which he told the President, according to his testimony, that she had signed the affidavit and that he was continuing to work on getting her a job. In both cases, Jordan testified, the President said, "Good."

The next day Jordan applied a little of what he calls the "Jordan magic" to close the deal on Lewinsky's job. On that day Lewinsky interviewed in New York City with a top executive of MacAndrews & Forbes Holdings Inc., billionaire Ron Perelman's umbrella company, but the executive decided she was unsuited for any opening. (Jordan is on the board of Revlon, a MacAndrews subsidiary.) Lewinsky reported to Jordan that the interview went "very poorly." So Jordan called Perelman. "I have spent a good part of my life learning institutions and people, and in that process, I have learned how to make things happen," he explained to the grand jury. "And the call to Ronald Perelman was a call to make things happen, if they could happen." (He also made three calls to the White House that day.) According to Perelman, Jordan touted Lewinsky as a "bright young girl who I think is terrific." It was the first time in the 12 years Jordan had served as a Revlon director that he had called to recommend someone for a job.

By the end of the day, Revlon called Lewinsky for an interview. On Jan. 9, she met with one executive from MacAndrews and two from Revlon. Within hours, Lewinsky was informally offered a job. She informally accepted and reported the news to Jordan. He immediately informed Currie and Clinton: "Mission accomplished." But Lewinsky still needed references, and Clinton reached down into the White House staff to make sure Lewinsky would get a favorable one. In the end, Revlon withdrew the job offer after the scandal broke.

During his Jones deposition on Jan. 17, Clinton was barraged with questions about Lewinsky. After the interrogation was finished, he called Currie and summoned her to the White House the following day, a Sunday. In the meeting, Currie testified, Clinton made a series of statements about himself and Lewinsky. "You were always there when she was there, right? We were never really alone. Monica came on to me, and I never touched her, right?"

None of them were right, but Currie felt "the President wanted her to agree with them," the report says. Starr charges that Clinton, worried Currie might be called for a deposition, was engaging in witness tampering. Clinton lawyer David Kendall rejects the charge, arguing that Currie was not a witness in any proceeding at the time (she was never called in the Jones matter). Clinton, in his August grand-jury testimony, conceded that Currie "may have felt some ambivalence about how to react" to his words. He said he had always tried to prevent her from learning of the affair. "[I] did what people do when they do the wrong thing," he said. "I tried to do it where nobody else was looking at it."

Three days later the scandal broke. . . .

The President denied the affair on television and in one-on-one conversations with aides who, perhaps believing the lie, repeated it endlessly when spinning the press and testifying before the grand jury. He used the power of the Executive Branch—the White House megaphone and the counsel's office—to attack Starr and impede his investigation with a series of privilege claims that were rejected by the courts. Through such tactics, the independent counsel's report claims, Clinton "abused his constitutional authority."

The charge echoes the second article of impeachment passed by the House in 1974, the one that charged Richard Nixon with "abuse of power." That count, an especially eloquent and sorrowful passage in the impeachment record, accused Nixon of no specific crime but rather of acting "in a manner contrary to his trust as President and subversive of constitutional government, to the great prejudice of the cause of law and justice and to the manifest injury of the people of the United States." Such abuse of power goes to the heart of the framers' conception of high crimes and misdemeanors, by which they meant offenses against the state and injuries to the Republic itself. Does Clinton's conduct reach that level?

Anyone with children may easily say yes. Yet clearly, nothing Clinton did sinks to the depths of what Nixon did, such as using the IRS to hound opponents and dispatching the CIA to thwart an FBI investigation. The claim that Clinton abused the counsel's office by invoking privilege claims is "nonsense," said White House counsel Charles Ruff, a respected former Watergate prosecutor and U.S. Attorney. "He did so on my advice. I went to the President and said the independent counsel is seeking to intrude into the legitimate, confidential discussions you have with your lawyers and that your senior staff have among themselves. It is your obligation as the President to protect the core constitutional interests of the presidency."

Some constitutional scholars argue that Clinton's more frivolous privilege claims injured the presidency, because Supreme Court rejection of the claims narrowed the circle of confidants any President can count on. But whatever the merits of the ploy, it is to Nixonian abuse as the Berkshires are to the Rockies.

What's more, Clinton's entire campaign of lies and obstructions in 1998 was designed to combat an investigation that Clinton—and many other Americans—viewed as fundamentally illegitimate. The only justification for Starr's probe of the Lewinsky affair—the reason [Attorney General] Janet Reno authorized it—was an alleged pattern of obstruction that Starr said stretched back to the Whitewater case.

Starr believes that Jordan and other Clinton pals steered some $540,000 in consultant contracts to former Associate Attorney General Webster Hubbell in exchange for his silence about an Arkansas land deal Starr was investigating. Starr saw the same pattern in Jordan's attempts to steer Lewinsky into a job. But Hubbell is barely mentioned in Starr's report. The independent counsel repeats the Hubbell allegation but does not explore it, or any other aspect of Whitewater. (Starr says he has not decided "what steps to take, if any," in referring any other matters to Congress.) The report is also silent on Travelgate and the White

House's alleged misuse of FBI files, implying that no impeachable offenses have been uncovered in those matters. As Clinton's defenders like to say, Starr spent four years and $40 million trying to prove substantive presidential wrongdoing, came up dry, and then used Linda Tripp's tapes to set a trap to catch the President in sordid personal behavior. Clinton's obstruction of justice—shameful though it may have been—amounted to trying to wriggle out of that trap.

Ken Starr's report, though lacking the balance of Watergate independent counsel Leon Jaworski's effort 24 years ago, does one thing quite clearly: it offers a portrayal of a President who seems cunning but emotionally vacant, a man wasting his talents and powers on an empty affair with a woman who was in many ways still a child. Public revulsion may yet drive Clinton from office—not because he has been proved a Nixonian crook but because he has been proved an X-rated cartoon.

"From the point of view of the law and the Constitution, the Lewinsky scandal is almost eerily like Watergate."

The Lewinsky Scandal Is Comparable to Watergate

David Frum

In the fall of 1998 the House Judiciary Committee met to consider impeachment proceedings against President Bill Clinton, following their receipt of a report by independent counsel Kenneth Starr. Starr had accused Clinton of impeachable offenses of perjury and obstruction of justice while attempting to conceal an affair with a White House intern. The only previous time in the twentieth century the committee had seriously considered impeaching a sitting U.S. president was in 1974, when it approved impeachment articles against Richard Nixon for his part in the Watergate scandal. In the following viewpoint, David Frum argues that strong similarities exist between the two presidential scandals. Both involved suborning of perjury, the refusal to provide full disclosure of past actions to Congress or the public ("stonewalling"), and the abuse of government intelligence and security agencies. Frum is a conservative political commentator and contributing editor to the *Weekly Standard*.

As you read, consider the following questions:
1. How has the luridness of the charges against Clinton actually helped the president, according to Frum?
2. What are some of the similarities between the actions of Nixon and Clinton, according to the author?

Weirdly enough, the very grossness of President Clinton's misconduct has proven to be his best defense. The details of Kenneth Starr's report to Congress are so lurid that it's hard at first to see past them (this is almost certainly the first government document in history whose readers have flipped past the executive summary to get to the footnotes). And by apologizing again and again for an "inappropriate" relationship with Monica Lewinsky, the president helps to keep attention focused on the mesmerizing smuttiness of his affair. That way, attention is diverted from the president's hanging offense—his unrepentant lying under oath.

Parallels with Watergate

What the Clinton team most wants to go unnoticed are the parallels between the Clinton scandals of the 1990s and the Nixon scandals of the 1970s. But that parallelism is so glaring that Clinton defenders can no longer avoid acknowledging it, if only for the purpose of denying it. . . .

What was Watergate about? At bottom, it was an attempt by a president to conceal his wrongdoing by corrupting the institutions of government. And what is the Lewinsky affair about? The very same thing. Yes of course the details of the two scandals vary: Details always do. Yes, too, the tone and style of the two scandals, and of the two presidents, could not differ more. Watergate was grand opera; Lewinsky is *Oh! Calcutta!* But from the point of view of the law and the Constitution, the Lewinsky scandal is almost eerily like Watergate. All unhappy coverups, it turns out, are alike.

In both cases, the president suborned perjury: Nixon from the Watergate burglars, Clinton from Monica Lewinsky. In both cases, the president eventually found himself blackmailed by those he had suborned: James McCord and the Watergate burglars wanted cash; Monica demanded a fancy job in New York (*not* as somebody's administrative assistant). In both cases, the president tampered with witnesses. Nixon tried to coax John Dean into lying; Clinton coached Betty Currie.

Convenient Amnesia

Even more striking, in both cases, perjury often manifested itself in the form of too-convenient amnesia: President Clinton swore that he could not remember ever being alone with Monica except when she delivered pizza to him; Nixon aide Dwight Chapin went to prison for six months for his failure to recall Donald Segretti's 1972 dirty-tricks campaign. Chapin's fate was sealed by Charles F.C. Ruff, now President Clinton's White House counsel and then a Watergate special prosecutor, who persuaded the Supreme Court not to hear an appeal. Chapin's defense, like Clinton's today, was that he provided the grand jury with legally accurate answers to ambiguous questions.

In the Lewinsky scandal as in Watergate, the president's subordinates illegally leaked private information about perceived enemies. It was for having Daniel Ellsberg's psychiatric records stolen and then disseminated that Charles Colson went to prison; we are still waiting to see what will happen to the Clinton Defense Department officials who leaked to the *New Yorker* information from Linda Tripp's confidential Pentagon personnel records.

Then as now, the president baffled his subordinates by stonewalling when it seemed that a swift confession and apology might still have saved him. Nixon stonewalled because he knew that full disclosure of his role in the Watergate burglary would lead to the exposure of even more glaring illegalities: the wiretapping of journalists and mistrusted staffers, the illegal campaign donations, the Ellsberg break-in. Clinton stonewalled for reasons we can still only surmise.

Then as now, the president and his men insisted that their troubles had nothing to do with their own actions and were entirely the work of malicious, out-of-control prosecutors. As the Nixon White House complained in June 1973, suggestions in the press that the president knew of the coverup

appear to be part of a careful coordinated strategy by an individual or individuals determined to prosecute a case against the President in the press using innuendo, distortions of fact and outright falsehood. This manipulation of the press involves an unprecedented assault on judicial and administrative due process. Its objective, stated in the simplest terms, is to destroy the President.

And then as now, in the last resort both presidents looked the nation in the eye and flat-out lied—Nixon unctuously, Clinton brazenly.

Abuse of Government Agencies

But the Starr report reveals an even more disturbing parallel: the abuse of the federal government's intelligence and security agencies. Section XI-C3 of the Starr report, subtitled "Whatever Just Happened Didn't Happen," tells the following amazing story. On Saturday, December 6, 1997—the day after the president learned that Monica Lewinsky had appeared on the list of potential witnesses in the Jones case—Monica showed up at the northwestern gate of the White House at 10 in the morning with a parcel of gifts for the president. She had been told that the president would be meeting with his lawyers and that she should leave the gifts with Betty Currie. But Currie could not immediately be found. As Lewinsky cooled her heels at the gatehouse, a guard let slip that the president was in fact meeting with another woman. "Livid," the report says, Lewinsky stormed off and telephoned and "berated" Currie. Two hours later, she was called back to the White House for her first meeting with the president in two months. He was, she happily e-mailed a friend, unusually affectionate with her. And he promised to prod Vernon Jordan to find her a job.

While the president was mollifying Monica, Betty Currie was warning the gatehouse guards that the president was so angry about their blabbing that he wanted somebody fired. The president himself called the watch commander into the Oval Office for a dressing down—and then demanded the guards keep their mouths shut about the morning's event. The watch commander returned to the gatehouse and ordered that no record of the incident be kept.

The events are so richly absurd—one woman in the president's office, another woman banging at the door; the president smilingly calming the angry woman and then chewing out his big-mouthed guards as soon as he has shooed her out the door—that it's possible to lose sight of their real meaning. After months of being nothing more than an irritating nuisance, Monica had suddenly became a potential danger. If Monica testified truthfully in the Paula Jones suit, it would strengthen Jones's case—and maybe encourage other women to come forward. It was urgently important that Monica be persuaded to perjure herself, and the Secret Service officers' indiscretion had complicated that task. An honest entry in the log book about Monica's appearance, gifts, and temper tantrum would make things even more complicated: It would offer substantial evidence that Monica and the president were lying when they disavowed any sexual relationship between them. So the log had to be doctored. And here the story stops being funny. Just as Richard Nixon urged the CIA to lie to the FBI to shut down the Watergate investigation, so Clinton was urging the Secret Service to engage in deception to shut down the Paula Jones lawsuit. He was, in other words, annexing the Secret Service to his own personal obstruction of justice.

"..'CHRISTMAS'?..NO... I'M THE GHOST OF IMPEACHMENTS PAST..."

Bill Schorr. Reprinted with permission from United Feature Syndicate, Inc.

Perhaps the most important political question posed by Watergate was this: For whom do the security forces of the United States work? Are they the president's henchmen, obliged to obey his every command on the theory (as Nixon memorably phrased it) that "When the president does it, that means it is not illegal"? Or do they owe their loyalty to the law and the Constitution? Watergate affirmed that it was the second course that is the correct answer, but President Clinton and his party apparently require a reminder.

Scandals and the Democratic Party

Perhaps his party needs it even more than he does. Ever since Watergate, the Democrats have basked in unprecedented moral self-regard. This is actually quite an anomalous situation. Before 1970, it was the Democrats—the party of the urban machines and the one-party South—who were usually thought of as the more crooked of the two great parties. It must have taken considerable humbug for Democrats who remembered how Kennedy had won in 1960 (the $5-a-vote West Virginia primary win; the ballot stuffing in Chicago) and how Johnson wiretapped his political enemies in 1968 to summon up a great whoop of indignation at the news that the '72 Nixon campaign had rifled the Democratic National Committee's files. But largely thanks to Watergate, since 1972 the Democrats have become the nice-people's party: the party of genteel good-government reformers, earnest schoolteachers, and Episcopalian bishops.

The Clinton scandals ought to cause the nice people to rethink. The scandals have exposed Clinton's supporters in Congress and the country as willing to condone law-breaking in some ways more blatant than Nixon's: Nixon at least never personally perjured himself before a grand jury. And they have called into question the morality not just of a single man but of an entire administration: While two of Nixon's cabinet officers (attorney general John Mitchell; commerce secretary Maurice Stans) were convicted of crimes, five of Clinton's officers are now under the shadow of the law. . . .

The Power of Fact

But it is going to take more than allegations to make the nice people rethink. One of the great lessons of the Clinton scandals is the brute power of fact. Washington insiders, privy to all the details that proximity to power brings, have presumed Clinton guilty of lying under oath since January [1998] and have condemned him for it. But it's only since August— when Clinton moved from being a presumed liar to a confessed one—that the nation's disgust for the man has begun to catch up to the capital's. For those who had followed the Lewinsky matter closely, Clinton's admission changed nothing; for everybody else, it changed everything.

The same will be true of the terms of Clinton's eventual punishment. It is not because Nixon was indelibly disgraced that he was forced to resign; it is because he was forced to resign that he is indelibly disgraced. If Clinton holds on to office, the public will very reasonably infer that the evidence was not there that would justify removing him. An administration that ought to be discredited as corrupt will instead slide into the history books as "controversial." Censure, censure plus a fine—neither of these will mean anything.

In fact, given Clinton's amazing ability to "accept responsibility" in one breath and claim innocence in the next, any punishment less than impeachment will be seized on by him as both an escape and carte blanche to continue lying, stonewalling, and obstructing justice in the two years remaining to him as president.

This is a political as well as a legal danger. For not until Clinton has been disgraced will his party be discredited for nominating and defending him. If there are any Republicans who imagine that they can eke out a greater political advantage by letting the Clinton scandals dribble on without a resolution than by proving perjury and obstruction in the Senate, they are deluding themselves. Clinton said early on that there could be only one survivor of the struggle between him and Ken Starr, and he was right. If the case against Clinton is somehow not borne out, the sleaze of the past eight months will unfairly but ineluctably splash back on those who have accused him.

The appetites that led Clinton into perjury and obstruction are so ludicrous and so pathetic that it is hard for Americans to see the perjury and obstruction as criminal. But crimes are crimes, whether the person responsible for them is in the end a sinister figure or a sad one. And in a republic of laws, crimes must be punished. The alternative is to blur forever the force of law and to leave Clinton's example intact as a permanent temptation to future presidents.

> *"This president has subverted our system of justice . . . , debased our politics, vulgarized our culture, and brought a totalitarian impulse to our government."*

Clinton's Numerous Scandals Show Him Unfit to Be President

Robert H. Bork

Robert H. Bork is an author and former federal judge. His books include *Slouching Toward Gomorrah: Modern Liberalism and American Decline*. In the following viewpoint, he argues that President Bill Clinton's numerous scandals, which extend far beyond the ones for which he was impeached in 1998, demonstrate his unfitness to hold the office of president. The president has consistently abused the power of his position and has demonstrated his unwillingness to be truthful to the American people and respectful of the law. Failure to impeach Clinton would mark a decline in America's values and in its standards for future presidents, Bork contends.

As you read, consider the following questions:

1. What do President Clinton's adulteries reveal about his character, according to Bork?
2. In what respects, in the author's view, does Clinton fit the medical definition of a sociopath?
3. Is Clinton a cause or a symptom of America's decline, in Bork's opinion?

Reprinted from Robert H. Bork, "Counting the Costs of Clintonism," *The American Spectator*, November 1998, by permission of the author.

The one hilarious moment in the sad and disgusting Clinton saga came at a fundraiser in Cincinnati. Pursued by his own manifold sins, lies, and impeachable offenses, the president managed a straight face as he assured the audience that the real scandal was a "Washington obsessed with itself instead of America." This, from a man whose self-absorption is legendary, if not pathological, at least deserves an Oscar for best self-parody.

We have come, at long last, to the end of the Clinton presidency. Whether he is removed from office or continues as a disdained and powerless figurehead, he is through. But the difference between impeachment and political impotence is crucial. It will be a test of the American people. If the head of the most corrupt and malign administration in our history is suffered to remain in office, however crippled, it will be a clear sign that we have turned a corner, that American morality, including but not limited to our political morality, is in free fall.

It is time to reckon the costs to America, so far, of this squalid and probably criminal administration. That the president has committed "high crimes and misdemeanors" is indisputable but not the worst of the wounds he has inflicted upon his office and the nation. The damage is enormous, cuts deep, and may be irreversible.

This president has subverted our system of justice and the ideal of the rule of law, debased our politics, vulgarized our culture, and brought a totalitarian impulse to our government. The really bad news, however, is that unless we display in the future far more care and attention than we did in 1992 and 1996, we will repeat our mistakes and elect more unprincipled demagogues.

Clinton Scandals and the Rule of Law

The rule of law is subverted when law itself, and the institutions that guard the law, are seen as no more than a means, or sometimes an obstacle, to power. The Department of Justice's fate was virtually sealed at the outset when a complaisant Janet Reno was named attorney general but real power lodged in the president's confidante, and now convicted felon, Webster Hubbell. Of the many partisan acts, the most outrageous is Ms. Reno's refusals, in plain violation of the law, to seek an independent counsel to investigate various campaign finance scandals linked to Clinton and Al Gore. Both Louis Freeh, the FBI director, and Charles La Bella, Reno's own designated investigator, say it is essential to appoint an independent counsel to probe the most serious of the suspected violations: the Asian and Chinese money that poured into Clinton's reelection campaign. As the coils tighten around Clinton the department may recover more of its integrity and Reno may ask for an independent counsel, although she has stalled for so long that the trail is frozen over.

While he was en route to prison, the president's aides and friends, largely at Clinton's urging, procured well over $700,000 for Hubbell as fees for "consulting" he could not possibly perform. Hubbell (consequently?) did not give the cooperation he had promised to independent counsel Kenneth Starr. Then too there were the Travel Office firings to make room for Clinton cronies, the misuse of the FBI to suggest Travel Office staff criminality, the removal of Vincent Foster's files from his office the night of his suicide, the transfer of at least 900, and possibly many more, raw FBI files (mostly about Republicans) to the White House, an FBI tipoff to the White House about an investigation, and Justice's opposition in court to the independent counsel's investigation.

Investigations have been frustrated by the shredding of documents, the withholding of files under subpoena, witnesses taking the Fifth Amendment or fleeing the country, and a spectacularly rapid spread of amnesia among administration personnel, a plague highly convenient to the White House. A journalist says witnesses recall matters very well when they talk to him, but then go before congressional committees and are unable to remember anything.

The Starr Investigation

The processes of justice have been savaged by the "war" on Kenneth Starr conducted by Bill and Hillary, ignobly abetted by sundry White House lackeys. The object is to delegitimize Starr's investigation and cast doubt upon his report. This is the moral, if not the legal, equivalent of an obstruction of justice. The war, despite its patent untruths, has partially succeeded. Starr, the mildest and most judicious of men, is now believed by a sizable number of Americans to be a rabid partisan. There are moments when one wishes he were.

Thanks to Starr, however, we now know the truth about Clinton's sexual depravity and lies. Despite the eely writhings and Rube Goldberg arguments of his lawyers, it is now absolutely clear that Clinton lied under oath several times in the Paula Jones case and also before the grand jury, and lied to the American people both in denying sex in January [1998] and admitting an "improper relationship" in August. When a president lies under oath he subverts a core constitutional duty of seeing that the laws are faithfully executed—in fact, he attempts to ensure that the laws are not faithfully executed—and thereby commits a clearly impeachable offense. Evidence of witness tampering and obstruction of justice is abundant. To cite but one example, Clinton obviously coached Monica Lewinsky to deny sex and then sat by as his lawyer pressed upon the court an affidavit by her that Clinton knew to be a lie.

Clinton partisans blame Starr for diminishing the legal rights of the presidency. How Starr can be blamed for the courts' rejections of claims put in play by the administration is a mystery. Clinton's assertions of executive privilege had been rejected unanimously by the Supreme Court in the Nixon tapes case. The invention of a "protective function privilege" for the Secret Service was merely laughable. The president's lawyers and the Department of Justice which supported those frivolous claims surely knew they hadn't a legal leg beneath them. Their assertions were another example of disrespect for law and abuse of the judicial process for the sole purpose of delay. They were not defending presidential prerogatives; they were defending the person of Bill Clinton. The legal terrain has not changed: What the presidency had before, the presidency has now.

Debased Politics

Clinton has also debased our politics. Misguided party loyalty has required Democrats to defend a man they know to be indefensible: dishonest, sexually depraved, and an incorrigible liar. Such behavior might have been expected of old-time Chicago aldermen, even regarded as admirable by a mobster's henchmen. For the men and women of Congress, however, loyalty to a corrupt and wicked leader can only destroy their personal and institutional honor. During the investigation of Richard Nixon, a great many Republicans turned on their president when the facts warranted it. Today's Democrats should reflect that those Republicans who fought to the last ditch died in it.

Abusing the Public Trust

One could go on—and on—enumerating Bill Clinton's lies under oath; together they amount to an abuse of the public trust, because together they amount to a concerted attempt to undermine the legal process. But Clinton has abused the public trust in a more fundamental way, too. He engaged in a shameless and sustained attempt, from January 21 [1998] on, to lie to the American people, to conceal, to obstruct all efforts to uncover the truth. These efforts reflect an utter lack of concern for the nation's well-being. Bill Clinton has acted for the past year on his deepest beliefs: that law is merely politics, that the truth is merely spin, that an oath is merely rhetoric, that justice is merely power. These doctrines are deeply corrosive of free government. They corrupt us and degrade our constitutional order in a profound way. This fundamental disdain for his presidential oath is Bill Clinton's highest crime and misdemeanor. And the remedy for high crimes and misdemeanors is impeachment.

William Kristol, *Newsweek*, December 21, 1998.

Clinton has inflicted enormous injury to the nation's character and culture. The president has established a mind-boggling record of adulteries. He is to infidelity what Cal Ripken is to baseball, except that Ripken ended his record streak voluntarily. American popular culture is already sex-drenched, and the example of the president reinforces the notion that sex has no moral overtones but is merely one more form of indoor recreation, akin to video games.

That is what makes so depressing the liberal mantra "it's just about sex." Quite aside from the fact that impeachment will not be "about sex" (but rather about perjury, obstruction of justice, etc.), sex is not irrelevant to the fitness of this man for the presidency. His sexual habits are a clue to his character and, according to the Starr report's footnotes, the clues are damning. They reveal a man whose tastes are, to put it gently, very kinky, and whose entire philosophy of the subject is immediate and reckless self-gratification. Yet we are urged to emulate European sophistication about the matter. Acceptance of Clinton's behavior is not sophisticated but decadent. Apparently sexual morality ought to flow east rather than west, though it must be acknowledged that decadence has already established a considerable beachhead here.

Nor should we accept the argument that sex is a "private" matter; the only persons legitimately concerned are Bill Clinton's family. We countenance no such public-private distinction for anyone else. Imagine a Chief Justice of the United States (not the current one) sexually serviced in his chambers by a 22-year-old female law clerk. The man would be impeached and out of office in a flash. No one would suggest we draw a veil of "privacy" over that behavior. Such conduct tells us about the man's lack of judgment and moral balance, and we would surely conclude that important affairs must not be left in his hands. When the offender is the president of the United States, all the greater should be our determination to be quit of him.

The president's incessant lying (as Mary McCarthy said of Lillian Hellman, every word he utters is a lie, including "and" and "the") inevitably diminishes respect for truth telling, even under oath. The tactic of delay, leaks of bits and pieces of the bad news, have had their intended effect. The public becomes bored with the topic of Clinton's behavior, and hence inured to it. Lying and vice come to seem the normal practice of men. Clinton has numbed our moral sense. Whether, with his passing, that sense can be reawakened remains an open question.

There is, as well, more than a whiff of totalitarianism about the Clinton White House. From the beginning in Arkansas, Clinton behaved, and required others to behave, as if he was the only person that really mattered. He used Arkansas state troopers and the federal Secret Service to abet his sexual appetites or hide his slaking of those appetites.

Supposed friends like Lani Guinier were dropped completely once their usefulness ended. He ignored social norms while developing a high degree of plausibility in the rhetoric that disguised his actions. In accordance with his "scorched earth" policy, enemies, critics, and witnesses are ruthlessly smeared, from Gennifer Flowers to Kathleen Willey to Scott Ritter to Ken Starr. Even those who might judge him adversely in the future, like the eminently decent Henry Hyde, are attacked with leaks. One begins to see why the White House wanted the raw FBI files: they are a reservoir of damaging information and misinformation that can be used to destroy others.

Clinton's Character

We are told that the president is filled with remorse and has repented. That is obviously false. The behavior he displays goes back for at least thirty years, but he never repented or promised reform until impeachment loomed. The dominant emotions displayed in his August 17 [1998] faux *mea culpa* was not contrition but fury at having been caught and brought to account, hatred of his adversaries, particularly Kenneth Starr, and an utter inability to understand how a man as wonderful as himself could be imagined to have real faults. Even in his address to the National Prayer Breakfast, Clinton coupled his words of contrition with the promise of a strong legal defense to be conducted by his attorneys. That nullified any statement of contrition. One cannot be accepted as a repentant liar if he denies lying and continues to lie.

There is a name for people like that: sociopaths. The *Merck Manual* of 1992 states that sociopaths

> characteristically act out their conflicts and flout normal rules of social order. These persons are impulsive, irresponsible, amoral, and unable to forgo immediate gratification. They cannot form sustained affectionate relationships with others, but their charm and plausibility may be highly developed and skillfully used for their own ends. They tolerate frustration poorly, and opposition is likely to elicit hostility, aggression, or serious violence. Their antisocial behavior shows little foresight, and is not associated with remorse or guilt, since these people seem to have a keen capacity for rationalizing and for blaming their irresponsible behavior on

others. Frustration and punishment rarely modify their behavior or improve their judgment and foresight. . . .

That definition fits Clinton to a T. Given power, the sociopath will display totalitarian tendencies. Clinton does. They are also likely to be demagogues. Clinton is.

Cause or Symptom?

It would be comforting to believe that this presidency is an aberration from which we will recover rather than a permanent and dangerous lowering of the qualifications we seek in a president. For that reason, we must ask whether Bill Clinton is a cause or a symptom. The answer is that he is both. He is a cause in that he has damaged our justice system, corrupted our political culture, debased our thoughts and language, and lowered our moral standards. But he is also a symptom of the combined effects of the spirit of 1968 and of our exploding media technology. The '68 generation believed that its moral superiority and purity of motive absolved it of any need for truth and decent behavior. Those people were, and many remain, antinomians, convinced that since they have been touched by the grace of radical politics, they are freed of normal restraints. This, too, has worked a deep corruption in the nation. People who are not in the least radical, or even interested in politics, eagerly accept the pleasures made possible by collapsing restraints. This, in turn, protects Clinton because the collapse of moral barriers means acceptance of moral relativism, and that means a refusal to judge the behavior of others. A journalist who has talked to people across the nation says the standard response to the scandal is, "Of course what he did is wrong, but who am I to judge?"

Clinton may be more typical of our future than of our past. Now, more than ever, the American public responds to politicians as it does to popular entertainers. Think of Clinton as [pop singer] Madonna. He may fade as she has; with any luck he may disappear completely. But, as with Madonna, there will be other Clintons, dismaying as that is to contemplate. [Sociologist] David Riesman once wrote that as the public loses competence to judge merits, it values "sincerity," which it believes, quite erroneously, that it is able to judge.

Clinton has learned to fake sincerity; others will too.

We must choose between reforming ourselves through Clinton's impeachment or continue our decline by ratifying his behavior, thereby notifying future presidents that almost all bars are down. If we ratify, our tomorrows will be even more wrenching than would impeachment today.

"*The right's remarkable promotion of the 'Clinton scandals'. . . represents . . . the systematic use of propaganda and disinformation to destabilize a sitting U.S. president.*"

Clinton's Scandals Have Been Exaggerated by Political Opponents

Robert Parry

In a January 1998 interview, Hillary Clinton argued that the brewing sex scandal surrounding President Bill Clinton was the product of a "vast right-wing conspiracy." In the following viewpoint, Robert Parry argues that her contention was not far off the mark. Since 1990, conservative political opponents of Clinton have financed and publicized numerous lurid allegations of sexual and political scandals against the Arkansas governor who was elected president in 1992. Parry argues that many of the stories of Clinton's misdeeds as governor and president have been exaggerated or even fabricated as part of an effort to discredit him and drive him from office. Their actions raise critical questions as to how scandals are created and exploited by political operatives. Parry is a journalist and editor of *iF Magazine*.

As you read, consider the following questions:
1. Who have been the sources of sexual allegations against Clinton, according to Parry?
2. What was the "Arkansas Project," according to Parry?

Reprinted from Robert Parry, "Was Hillary Right?" *In These Times*, June 14, 1998, with permission.

With the Republican House majority at risk, House speaker Newt Gingrich is abandoning his kinder, gentler persona and is returning to his old partisan self. Gingrich is instructing Republicans to refer to the "Clinton scandals" as "crimes" and to use other buzz words like "stonewall" or "Watergate.". . .

The key to Gingrich's strategy will be getting the public to accept that President Clinton is indeed a corrupt politician on par with—or worse than—Richard Nixon.

In its frighteningly glib manner, the Washington news media have already bought into that comparison. The same press corps that quickly grew bored with the complex scandals of the Reagan-Bush era and seems to have forgotten Nixon's deep bag of Watergate-era dirty tricks just can't get enough of Monica and Paula and "the White House in crisis."

Yet, while going wild over every fresh Clinton accusation, the national press corps has given short shrift to recent dramatic disclosures that many of these "scandals" were, in fact, fabricated by well-financed conservative propagandists. Others, meanwhile, sprang from opportunists hoping to tap into right-wing slush funds.

An Anti-Clinton Conspiracy

In January [1998], when Hillary Clinton responded to the Monica Lewinsky meltdown by blaming a "vast right-wing conspiracy," the Washington Press Corps mocked her as some *X-Files* fantasist. Washington journalists have sniffed, too, at disclosures emanating from the internet magazine *Salon*, and elsewhere that trace hundreds of thousands of dollars in conservative money into the pockets of anti-Clinton investigators, operatives and witnesses.

Despite that collective media yawn, the history of Republicans exaggerating Clinton's misdeeds—sexual and otherwise, dates back at least to 1990 when Clinton fought a nasty gubernatorial campaign against Republican Sheffield Nelson. When Clinton stepped onto the National stage in 1992, many of his Arkansas enemies saw a new chance to hurt their nemesis and cash in with stories, some of which had grains of truth while others were complete fabrications.

In 1992, we now know, Republican moneymen were spreading around cash in hopes of securing some devastating sex stories. "A major contributor to Newt Gingrich's GOPAC [a political action committee] . . . importuned [me] to follow up on a story in a supermarket tabloid that suggested you [Clinton] had fathered a child with a Little Rock prostitute," wrote journalist David Brock in an "open letter to the president" in the April [1998] issue of *Esquire*.

Brock recently confirmed stories by the *New York Observer* and the *Chicago Sun-Times* that the GOPAC donor was Chicago financier Peter W. Smith. According to those accounts, Smith paid Brock $5,000, gave Arkansas state troopers Roger Perry and Larry Patterson $6,700 each, and funnelled tens of thousands more to lawyers and PR consultants to market the anti-Clinton stories.

Troopergate

Clinton's electoral victory did not give the Republicans much pause. "Eight months into your presidency, the dirty war was on again," Brock recalled. With Smith again helping to bankroll the operation, Brock soon was transcribing the troopers' salacious—and often improbable—accounts about the sex lives of both Bill and Hillary Clinton.

Those tales, which Brock now suspects were either grossly exaggerated or made up, became the basis for his December 1993 article in *The American Spectator* on Troopergate.

In the article, Brock also mentioned an alleged Clinton encounter with a woman named Paula at a Little Rock hotel in 1991. Weeks later, Paula Jones elbowed her way to national attention at a news conference at the Conservative Political Action Conference, an annual Washington trade show for right-wing entrepreneurs, whose booths were already bristling with Clinton-hating paraphernalia. Jones claimed to have been the "Paula" in question and insisted that Clinton had made a crude sexual advance in the hotel room.

Soon afterwards, Jones filed a lawsuit, but those financing it saw a larger goal in humiliating Clinton. In *Esquire*, Brock noted that "one of Jones' key legal advisers told me that he didn't necessarily believe her story of sexual harassment. . . . 'This is about proving Troopergate,' he told me gleefully."

Appearing on CNN's *Crossfire*, Brock acknowledged that

Hillary Clinton's charge about a "vast right-wing conspiracy" wasn't far off the mark. "There is a right-wing [apparatus] and I know what it is," Brock said. "I've been there, I was part of it and, yes, they were trying to bring down Bill Clinton by damaging him personally . . . by any means necessary."

Prompting Suspicions About Clinton

While the sex stories moved on one track, conservative operatives also churned ahead with tales of Clinton violently abusing power, both in Arkansas and Washington. In 1993–94, a rash of right-wing "investigative" articles appeared in conservative publications, such as the *Washington Times*, *American Spectator*, London *Sunday Telegraph* and *Wall Street Journal*. The stories depicted Arkansas as a dangerous Third World country terrorized by Clinton goons.

In one high-profile story, the *Wall Street Journal*'s editorial page suggested that *New Republic* writer L.J. Davis had been clubbed by Clinton operatives who then stole some of his Whitewater notes. It turned out that Davis had been downing martinis in a hotel bar at the time of the alleged attack and that no notes were missing.

Even more famously, Rush Limbaugh and other conservative voices began promoting suspicions about the suicide of White House Deputy Counsel Vincent Foster. Unsourced allegations claimed that Foster had died elsewhere and was transported to the park. The Foster and other "death squad" charges were summed up in a slick video called *The Clinton Chronicles* produced by a Christian right group, Citizens for Honest Government, and promoted by the Rev. Jerry Falwell on his *Old Time Gospel Hour*.

The Foster conspiracists got a boost when two Arkansas troopers of Troopergate fame, Roger Perry and Larry Patterson, asserted that a White House aide named Helen Dickey had called Little Rock in the late afternoon of July 20 [1993] with word that Foster had shot himself in the White House parking lot. Since the White House did not officially hear about Foster's death until after 9 P.M., the troopers' claim would mean that the details of the death must have been covered up and that the body indeed had been moved.

The troopers' account, however, collapsed when Dickey

testified that she did not learn about Foster's death until between 9 and 10 P.M., when she began calling family and friends. Her timing was backed by White House phone records—not to mention the absurdity of the idea that a daylight shooting could occur on White House grounds and not be noticed by thousands of tourists, journalists, bureaucrats and police.

Scott Stantis. Reprinted by permission of Copley News Service.

Even Starr, who conducted his own investigation of Foster's death, was forced to accept the overwhelming evidence that Foster had committed suicide at Fort Marcy Park. (Still, Starr took no legal action against the troopers, whose credibility remains important in Starr's expected sex-perjury charges against Clinton.)

The Money Trail

But the troopers' phony Foster claim helped unravel another secret about how the Clinton scandals had been knitted together. *Salon* investigative reporter Murray Waas discovered that Citizens for Honest Government "covertly paid more than $200,000 to individuals who made damaging allegations about President Clinton's personal conduct."

Larry Nichols, the Arkansas representative of Citizens for Honest Government, signed a contract in March 1995 with Perry and Patterson. The two troopers were to make statements challenging the official suicide findings, which they did in their account of the Dickey phone call. Waas says he discovered the contract when Perry began complaining that Nichols hadn't delivered the promised money.

But the Citizens' payoff and the money from GOPAC donor Smith were not the only conservative slush funds sloshing around Arkansas. Right-wing billionaire Richard Mellon Scaife dropped $1.8 million into another money bucket called the "Arkansas Project." Those funds flowed through the *American Spectator*. . . .

According to Waas and Jonathan Broder, some of that money went into the pocket of Starr's chief Whitewater witness, David Hale, the Arkansas judge who testified to Clinton's alleged misdeeds. In *Salon*, Waas and Broder detailed allegations that Hale was receiving cash and other gratuities from a conservative operative, sportsman Parker Dozhier, who was paid $48,000 by the Arkansas Project.

Salon quoted Dozhier's former live-in girlfriend, Caryn Mann, and her 17-year-old son, Joshua Rand, who described how Dozhier made cash payments of $500 or less to Hale when the former municipal judge stayed at Dozhier's cabin in Hot Springs, Ark. According to the story, Hale also got free lodging and use of Dozhier's car.

This disclosure created a problem for Starr, a conservative who has also worked closely with groups financed by Scaife. At the end of the Whitewater investigation, Starr had planned to accept a position subsidized by Scaife at Pepperdine University. After the *Salon* article, Starr renounced those appointments but refused to permit a Justice Department review of the Hale allegations.

The Whitewater Investigation

Despite the payoff charges, Hale remains the linchpin of a second set of allegations in Starr's expected impeachment report. A convicted con man who defrauded the Small Business Administration of $2 million, Hale is the only living witness to claim first-hand knowledge connecting Clinton to a Whitewater crime. Hale alleges that Clinton pressured him to approve a bogus $300,000 loan to Susan McDougal, a partner in the Whitewater real estate investment. Clinton denies the charge.

For nearly four years, Starr has sought corroboration of Hale's account. In doing so, the independent counsel applied extraordinary legal pressure on Susan McDougal and her late husband, Jim McDougal, both of whom insisted that Clinton had no involvement in the loan. But that was not an answer Starr would accept.

At the McDougals' fraud trial in 1996, Starr finally got his first piece of corroboration when a Hale business associate, William Watt, testified that he remembered Hale twice mentioning pressure from Clinton on the McDougal loan. The testimony extricated Watt from potential legal difficulties surrounding his work with Hale.

However, a review of newspaper clips reveals that two years earlier, Watt told *Newsday* that he had never heard Hale mention any pressure from Clinton. "The problem I have with [Hale's] scenario," Watt said, "is that he never once implied to one of us that he was getting pressured."

Nevertheless, Watt's revised recollection proved useful to Starr. The 1996 testimony helped convince a federal jury in Little Rock to convict the McDougals, along with Arkansas Gov. Jim Guy Tucker, giving Starr new leverage. Starr then offered the ailing Jim McDougal leniency if he finally would implicate Clinton. Fearing death in prison, McDougal agreed.

Pressuring Witnesses

Starr next turned on Susan McDougal, who was paraded around in an orange prison jump suit and shackles. Despite her disgrace, she wouldn't buckle. Indeed, she charged that Starr had put her in a Catch-22. He planned to indict her for perjury if she continued to tell the truth about Clinton's non-involvement. Only by lying and implicating Clinton, she said, could she avoid a perjury charge. So, Susan McDougal refused to testify at all and was jailed 18 months for contempt of court. Jim McDougal got a reduced sentence in exchange for incriminating the president but nevertheless died in prison last March [1998].

In May, Starr indicted Susan McDougal for criminal contempt again, a charge that could give her another five years in prison. Starr also played hardball with Clinton friend Webster Hubbell, indicting him on tax charges. In reaction, Hubbell claimed that Starr wanted him to perjure himself to implicate Clinton. Starr's prosecutors "can indict my dog, they can indict my cat, but I'm not going to lie about the president," declared Hubbell, who has already served a prison term for cheating his law firm in the '80s.

Congressional Republicans added to Hubbell's discomfort by releasing what they considered incriminating tapes Hubbell had made of private prison conversations with his wife and lawyers. It turned out, however, that the tapes had been edited to delete exculpatory comments about the Clintons and that the transcripts had been altered to add damaging words.

The Myth of Clinton's Drug Smuggling

Earlier in 1998, another long-running Arkansas myth exploded about Clinton's supposed connection to one more high crime: cocaine trafficking at an airport in Mena, Arkansas. The allegations linking Clinton to Mena rested heavily on the testimony of another infamous Arkansas trooper, L.D. Brown. This time, Brown claimed to have flown CIA-authorized drug flights out of Mena. Brown said he had mentioned the flights to Clinton.

Spurred on by Gingrich, the House Banking Committee conducted a two-year investigation into the allegations but failed to develop any evidence incriminating the president. "We haven't come up with anything to support these allegations concerning then-Governor Clinton," committee spokesman David Runkel says. Still, the committee is moving slowly on a formal report that would clear Clinton, a delay that allows conservatives to continue circulating the charge.

In his reporting, Waas discovered that the Mena allegations were another pricey part of the Arkansas Project. He wrote that private investigator Rex Armistead, who fed Mena information directly to Starr's office and into the Banking Committee, was paid $250,000 by the Scaife-funded project. According to Waas, Armistead held secret meetings with

Starr's deputy, W. Hickman Ewing Jr., with the contents of the discussions sometimes kept out of official files.

The Arkansas Project even tried to dig up dirt on a reporter whose findings undercut the Mena suspicions. After CNN correspondent John Camp challenged Brown's claims, Waas reported, Armistead launched an examination of Camp's personal life, even interviewing Camp's ex-wife.

The Larger Issue

Many Americans—from the left as well as the right—might feel that Clinton deserves whatever he gets because they disagree with his policies and don't like him personally. But there is a larger issue beyond Clinton: Can we allow well-funded political operatives accountable only to their ideological patrons to gain effective veto power over who governs in Washington simply by virtue of their capacity to defame?

Viewed in its totality, the right's remarkable promotion of the "Clinton scandals"—in league with a conservative special prosecutor and a Republican congressional majority—represents a political watershed: the systematic use of propaganda and disinformation to destabilize a sitting U.S. president.

Periodical Bibliography

The following articles have been selected to supplement the diverse views presented in this chapter. Addresses are provided for periodicals not indexed in the *Readers' Guide to Periodical Literature*, the *Alternative Press Index*, the *Social Sciences Index*, or the *Index to Legal Periodicals and Books*.

David M. Abshire
"Nixon, Reagan, and Clinton," *Vital Speeches*, July 1, 1999.

Joanne Barkan
"Democratic Questions," *Dissent*, Spring 1999.

Gloria Borger
"Considering Contempt," *U.S. News & World Report*, April 26, 1999.

Ann Coulter
"High Crimes," *National Review*, September 14, 1998.

E.J. Dionne Jr.
"The Toxic State of Politics," *Liberal Opinion*, March 1, 1999. Available from PO Box 880, Vinton, IA 52349.

Ronald Dworkin
"The Wounded Constitution," *New York Review of Books*, March 18, 1999.

Florence Graves with Jacqueline E. Sharkey
"Starr and Willey: The Untold Story," *Nation*, May 17, 1999.

Anthony Lewis
"Back to a Republican System," *New York Times*, July 6, 1999.

Richard Lowry
"The Partisans," *National Review*, December 31, 1998.

John O. McGinnis
"Impeachable Defenses," *Policy Review*, June/July 1999.

Lars-Erik Nelson
"Clinton and His Enemies," *New York Review of Books*, January 20, 2000.

Jay Nordlinger
"Watergate Babies," *National Review*, December 31, 1998.

Michael J. Sandel
"Watergate Baby," *New Republic*, October 26, 1998.

Arthur Schlesinger
"Partisan Impeachment for Private Acts Challenges the Constitution," *New Perspectives Quarterly*, Winter 1999.

Society
"Symposium: Crisis in the American Presidency," March/April 1999.

Jeffrey R. Toobin
"The Secret War in Starr's Office," *New Yorker*, November 15, 1999.

CHAPTER 4

What Reforms Can Prevent Political Corruption?

Chapter Preface

In 1971, in an attempt to curb the influence of money in politics, Congress passed the Federal Election Campaign Act (FECA). Strengthened in 1974 and amended in 1979, FECA remains the central legislation governing the financing of national elections. FECA set campaign spending limits and required public disclosure of the amount and source of campaign donations. The 1974 amendments set monetary limits on what people, political action committees (PACs), and political parties could contribute to political candidates, and established the Federal Election Commission (FEC) to enforce campaign finance rules.

The Supreme Court in 1976 overturned campaign spending limits as unconstitutional, arguing that such spending was a form of free speech protected by the First Amendment. They let stand contribution limits and disclosure requirements, however. Donations made to candidates and recorded by the FEC became known as "hard money."

However, individuals, corporations, and labor unions found that they could contribute unlimited amounts of money directly to national and state party committees for party-building activities such as voter registration and conventions. Such "soft money" is donated and spent beyond the purview of the FEC and is not supposed to endorse specific candidates. But parties and candidates have utilized millions of dollars of soft money for television advertisements that are designed to help specific federal candidates (without expressly saying "vote for" or "vote against" a specific candidate).

Many people agree that, because of this use of soft money and other legal loopholes, FECA has failed in its goal of reducing the potentially corrupting influence of private money on the nation's elections and politicians. Sharp disagreement exists, however, on how best to reform the system. The viewpoints in the following chapter examine some of the debates surrounding campaign finance and debate whether procedural reforms can restore public confidence in elections.

1

"The rise in unregulated money flowing into elections ha[s] disillusioned the public."

Private Campaign Contributions Should Be More Strictly Regulated

Part I: John B. Judis; Part II: Committee for Economic Development

The authors of the following two-part viewpoint contend that private financing of elections threatens the integrity of America's political system. In Part I, John B. Judis, an editor for the *New Republic* magazine, asserts that wealthy individuals and groups have a disproportionate influence on how candidates are elected. He examines reform proposals by Republican senator John McCain and former Democratic senator Bill Bradley. Part II of the viewpoint is by the Committee for Economic Development (CED), an independent public policy organization comprised of leading business and academic executives. McCain, Bradley, and the CED all propose banning or limiting both "soft money" contributions to political parties and independent "issue" advertisements.

As you read, consider the following questions:
1. What was the assumed basis for equality at America's founding, according to Judis?
2. What four general recommendations does the CED make on campaign finance reform?

Part I: From John B. Judis, "Cash Out," *The New Republic*, August 23, 1999. Copyright 1999 by The New Republic, Inc. Reprinted by permission of *The New Republic. Part II:* Reprinted from the Committee for Economic Development, Executive Summary of *Investing in the People's Business: A Business Proposal of Campaign Finance Reform*, 1999, with permission.

I

The outcome of the current contest for the [2000] Republican presidential nomination may be decided before any citizen votes in a primary or caucus. It will be determined by whichever candidate can get the highest number of wealthy people to write $1,000 checks. This is no way to run a democracy, and it is a result of our sorry system of campaign finance. Two presidential candidates, Democrat Bill Bradley and Republican John McCain, have addressed the flaws of this system and proposed remedies for them. . . .

America's original promise of political democracy was based on a premise of rough economic equality among the country's farmers and craftsmen, which, projected onto the political realm, would prevent the rise of tyranny and monopoly. But the growth of large-scale industry after the Civil War undermined this formula for success. Not only did it give the top tier of bankers and businessmen inordinate power over key economic decisions, it also gave them power, through their control of campaign finance, over government itself. During the twentieth century, there were two major efforts to reform the political system so that it could act as a public political counterweight to this private economic inequality. In 1907, Theodore Roosevelt sought to introduce public financing of campaigns but had to settle for barring direct corporate contributions. And, in 1974, in the midst of the Watergate scandal, Congress passed comprehensive reform measures, but they were undermined by perverse court decisions and by loopholes left in the legislation.

There are two ways in which our current system reinforces rather than counters this inequality of private economic power. First, most of the contributions to congressional and presidential primary candidates come from the nation's most wealthy individuals. In a study funded by the Joyce Foundation, researchers found that in the 1996 congressional elections, 81 percent of the donors had an annual family income of $100,000 or more, while 80 percent of Americans made no contributions at all to a candidate or political party. The Joyce study also discovered that contributors tend to be more conservative, more Republican, and more inclined to slash public services for the sake of a tax cut than the average voter. That's troubling when you consider that those who contribute gain inordinate influence over the political process and skew the results toward their own objectives. The current system also allows candidates to spend as much of their own money as they want, enabling fabulously rich individuals such as oil heir Michael Huffington and magazine heir Steve Forbes to wield far more influence over public debate than their wisdom or experience alone might entitle them to.

Second, there are the unregulated contributions that work their way back into elections. In 1979, to revitalize political parties, Congress began allowing them to raise unlimited and unrestricted "soft money" contributions to put toward "party-building" activities, such as voter registration. But, with the approval of the courts, parties have increasingly used this measure to garner huge contributions that can be used to directly influence election results—either through paying for overhead campaign expenses or through issue advertising. Soft money contributions are even more skewed by class than hard-money gifts to candidates. In 1996, 90 percent of the $203 million in soft money came from corporations, trade associations, and other business groups and businessmen. These kinds of spending were augmented by millions in independent expenditures that were not officially authorized by either candidates or parties and therefore escaped restrictions on disclosure and on the size of contributions. . . .

Proposed Reforms

McCain, with Democratic senator Russ Feingold, has sponsored legislation to address the second of these problems. McCain and Feingold want to ban soft money contributions to parties from corporations, unions, and individuals and to also ban the use of independent ads that specifically promote a candidate during the last 30 days before a primary and the last 60 days before a general election. Bradley's proposals echo those in McCain and Feingold's bill, but they also address the problems created by private financing of congressional elections. Bradley would have the public fund general elections and grant matching funds for contributions of $250 or less during primaries. He would also require television broadcasters to make free airtime available to candidates 60 days before an election. Bradley's proposal, which admittedly doesn't have to conform to the realities of today's Congress, would clearly go much further than McCain and Feingold in severing the tie between private wealth and public politics. Requiring taxpayer funds would certainly prove controversial, but, as the system continues to sour, citizens would have to weigh the money spent in public financing against the greater billions that special interests exact in subsidies and tax breaks as a result of their campaign contributions.

II

The American public believes that our campaign finance system is broken. The vast majority of citizens think that money threatens the basic fairness and integrity of our politics. Opinion surveys consistently show widespread public cynicism toward government and the electoral process. Skyrocketing campaign costs and the rise in unregulated money flowing into elections have disillusioned the public, who increasingly believe the interests of large donors, especially businesses, are being served rather than their own. These conditions produce distressingly low voter turnout, a decrease in electoral competition, and reduced trust in government.

CED is concerned about the influence of money in politics and the public's negative opinion of government and business. As business leaders, we are troubled by the mounting pressure for businesses to contribute to the campaigns their competitors support, as well as the dangers that real or perceived political corruption pose for business and the economy. We have therefore impartially reviewed our campaign finance system and issued the following findings and recommendations:

Findings

- *Money and fundraising have become too important and demanding in our political life.* House campaign expenditures now exceed $500,000 while average Senate expenditures have reached $3.8 million. To raise enough money to be competitive, candidates spend an inordinate amount of time fundraising, reducing the time they spend communicating their ideas and policy positions to constituents.

- *The high cost of campaigns and the burdens of fundraising have reduced competition and the pool of qualified candidates in federal elections.* The daunting financial requirements to launch a competitive candidacy discourage many qualified candidates from seeking office. In particular, challengers, who are consistently underfunded compared with incumbents, find the financial obstacles difficult to overcome. Incumbents, too, increasingly withdraw from public office. The result is less competition in elections and reduced voter choice.

- *The role of the small donor has declined.* Tremendous emphasis is placed on soliciting large individual and political action committees' (PAC) donations instead of acquiring broad-based support from smaller donors. Incumbents in particular benefit from large PAC donations, which are used to gain access to legislators. This relationship between PACs and members of Congress, and the reduced attention to small donors, reduces public confidence in their representatives' integrity, and discourages large segments of the population from participating in the electoral process.

John Branch/*San Antonio Express News.* Reprinted with permission.

- *Unregulated funds raised and spent in federal elections have increased dramatically.* Current campaign finance law and regulations have encouraged an explosion of unregulated money in elections. "Soft money" and candidate specific "issue" advertising are exempt from federal contribution limits and disclosure requirements. These devices allow large donations from a few sources to wield great influence in elections and increase the possibility of corrupt relationships between candidates and their supporters.

CED has determined that comprehensive reform of the campaign finance system is necessary to improve public trust in government and increase civic participation in the political process. After careful consideration of a wide variety of proposals, we issue the following recommendations, which we believe balance First Amendment protections of political speech with the need for regulation:

Recommendations

- *Eliminate Soft Money.* The use of "soft money" by national parties violates the basic principle that funds used to promote political candidacies should be subject to federal campaign finance laws. We recommend that Congress prohibit national party committees from soliciting, receiving and spending contributions not subject to the limitations and public disclosure requirements of federal law. Because eliminating soft money will reduce the ability of parties to support candidates, we propose allowing individuals to donate an additional $25,000 to national parties. CED also applauds the businesses who currently refuse to participate in the soft money system and encourages other business leaders, labor unions, and individuals to voluntarily work to reduce soft money.
- *Improve Candidate Access to Resources.* Candidates need the opportunity to raise the funds necessary to communicate their positions to the public without spending excessive time fundraising. To achieve this, we propose increasing the limit on individual contributions to federal candidates from $1,000 to $3,000 per candidate per election,

with an aggregate limit of $25,000 per individual to all candidates and PACs (in addition to the $25,000 aggregate limit to national parties). To enhance the role of small donors and provide challengers with increased access to resources, we propose publicly financed $2 for $1 matching funds for individual donations of up to $200 for congressional candidates who agree to voluntary spending limits.

- *Reduce the Fundraising "Arms Race" with Congressional Spending Limits.* We recommend inflation-adjusted spending limits in congressional campaigns for candidates who accept public financing. The limits must be generous enough to induce candidates to accept the financing, but stringent enough to moderate the growth in campaign costs. We recommend limits of $500,000 per election in House races, and $1 million plus $.50 times the number of voting-age citizens in the state for Senate races, supplemented for run-offs. These limits would be adjusted for candidates facing opponents who have not agreed to limits. Party committees would be allowed to supplement a candidate's resources up to the amount of the relevant spending limit if the candidate does not raise the full amount. We also recommend that Congress review the structure and staffing of the Federal Election Commission (FEC) and provide the resources necessary to administer such a program.

- *Reform Issue Advocacy.* We recommend that Congress expand the definition of "express advocacy" communications and require that these communications be completely financed by funds raised under federal contribution limits and reporting requirements. Express advocacy should include communications that occur within specified time periods before elections, refer to or feature a clearly identified federal candidate, and would be understood by a reasonable person to be encouraging others to support or oppose that candidate. Should the courts not accept such a broader definition, we recommend full public disclosure of spending and funding sources for such communications undertaken within a certain time period prior to an election.

We believe reform is necessary to achieve a more effective, participatory campaign finance and electoral system. These changes will produce more competitive elections, improve the quality of representation by elected officials, and promote public confidence in our political process.

| "*The big government approach to campaign finance reform . . . has failed in the past and is bound to fail in the future.*"

Private Campaign Contributions Should Not Be More Strictly Regulated

John Doolittle

John Doolittle, a Republican, represents California's fourth district in the House of Representatives. He is the sponsor of the Citizen Legislature and Political Freedom Act, which he describes in the following viewpoint. His proposed legislation would repeal all restrictions on campaign contributions and enable people to give as much money as they wished to political candidates, while providing for full public disclosure of all contributions. Such an approach is superior to greater federal restrictions and regulations advocated by other campaign finance reformers, he contends. He disputes the contentions that too much money is spent campaigning and that members of Congress are corrupted by campaign gifts.

As you read, consider the following questions:

1. What four false assumptions underlie the drive for greater federal regulation of elections, according to Doolittle?
2. What did the Supreme Court rule in the case of *Buckley v. Valeo*, according to the author?
3. How will political challengers benefit from no restrictions on campaign contributions, in Doolittle's opinion.

Reprinted from "More Regulation Is Not Answer to Campaign Finance Reform," article on John Doolittle's website at www.house.gov/doolittle.

Turn on the evening news any given night, and you are bound to hear one of the following "golden oldies" of campaign finance reform: "Campaigns are becoming too expensive." "Only millionaires can afford to run for office." Or "'Special interests' are buying votes with large contributions." These generalizations are usually followed by an interview with some earnest-looking advocate of "good government" who concludes that the system of financing campaigns needs to be "reformed."

Nowhere in these news reports are the clichés and platitudes that pepper the campaign finance debate thoroughly examined. For instance, how do we know that campaigns have become "too expensive"? Compared to what? And just what is the optimal cost of campaigns in a market economy?

Although no one is certain what problems truly exist with the current system, nearly everyone seems to have a solution. In fact, the professional reformers all seem to favor the same solution: more federal regulation.

Before Congress considers any legislative proposal to add to the campaign finance bureaucracy, it is imperative that we examine the underlying assumptions behind the drive for further federal regulation of campaign financing. Many of the core assumptions the would-be regulators make about campaign financing simply aren't true.

What assumptions of the regulators need to be challenged?

Four False Assumptions

• *False Assumption #1: We spend too much money on campaigns.* The regulators will throw a seemingly impressive statistic in your face: Congressional campaign spending reached $724 million for the 1994 elections, an all-time high. Yet this figure, without context, is meaningless.

Madison Avenue spent more than *four times* that amount— $3 billion—*advertising toiletries and cosmetics alone* in 1994. American consumers, as George Will has pointed out, spend more than twice as much on yogurt than what is spent annually on political advertising.

Regulators will argue that these comparisons are meaningless because far more people buy these consumer products than contribute to campaigns, but the bottom line is *election spending since 1980 has been fairly constant, fluctuating between .04% and .06% of gross domestic product.*

• *False Assumption #2: Candidates can freely spend their way to election.* Advocates of regulation, like Common Cause, in their ongoing attempt to equate *all* money with evil, would have you believe that the candidate who spends more money in a campaign—particularly those candidates who greatly out-spend their opponents—will always win the election. If this outcome were really the case, why didn't Steve Forbes win the 1996 Republican nomination for President? Why isn't Michael Huffington now the junior senator from California? Why didn't the higher-spending Democratic [Mark] Warner win a Virginia Senate seat last November 1996?

It is true that candidates—particularly challengers—re-quire large amounts of money to run effective campaigns. But as the failed candidacies of Forbes, Huffington and Warner demonstrate, money alone does not guarantee elec-tion. The electorate still must approve of a candidate's mes-sage or else that candidate will not win.

• *False Assumption #3: Members are bought and sold through campaign contributions.* Wrong again. If members were as corrupt as Common Cause wants the public to believe, then why doesn't that organization simply name the members it believes to be improperly influenced? Political scientist Her-bert E. Alexander of the University of Southern California has demonstrated that campaign contributions have little if any influence on the way members vote. Much more impor-tant factors, Alexander found, are constituents' interest, po-litical beliefs and party loyalties.

• *False Assumption #4: Greater government regulation offers the only solution to our campaign finance problems.* This is the most dangerous of the false assumptions. I agree that many problems exist with our system of campaign financing. Yet these problems—including the perpetual "money chase" that forces candidates to spend too much of their time fund-raising and the difficulty faced by challengers to raise the "seed money" necessary to knock off incumbents—can be traced di-rectly back to the Watergate-era reforms of the 1970s.

These regulations created today's problems by limiting the amount an individual can donate to a candidate to $1,000 per election—an amount that has never been indexed for inflation! As a result of this failed reform, candidates have been forced to spend an even greater amount of time fund-raising instead of being able to raise funds more efficiently through larger donations.

More Regulations Will Make Problems Worse

Unfortunately, despite clear evidence that the government's leap into regulating campaign financing caused the problems we experience today, advocates of greater regulation see this evidence as an excuse to impose even more stringent regulations upon campaign finances. These solutions, as embodied last [104th] Congress in the Senate's McCain-Feingold bill and the House's Smith-Shays proposal, would have only made existing problems worse. [Both bills limiting campaign contributions failed to pass.]

By ratcheting down even more the amount of money available per donor, these reforms would have forced candidates to spend an even greater amount of time grubbing for money. Such a result will exacerbate the appearance of corruption so often alleged by these regulators.

Additionally, by limiting the amount of money available to challengers, it will be even tougher to knock off incumbents. As we all know, incumbents enter elections with a whole range of advantages. They have taxpayer-paid staffs at their disposal to drum up media attention, travel frequently to their districts at taxpayer expense for official function, and create opinion pieces and television programs for their local media. While receiving these advantages, incumbents continue to receive their annual salaries. Many challengers must temporarily leave their jobs and forgo income during the same period.

To counter these inherent advantages of incumbency, challengers need money—*lots* of money. Unfortunately, current campaign finance laws greatly restrict their ability to raise this money. The limits on contributions force all candidates—incumbents and challengers alike—to spend even more time raising money.

Although this circumstance certainly inconveniences incumbents, they are generally able to raise the needed money throughout a two-year election cycle. Challengers, on the other hand, almost without exception, cannot commence fund-raising until the actual election nears.

And evidence from recent elections proves that challengers who spend a great deal of money are more competitive. In 1994, both successful senatorial challengers spent more to get their message out than would have been permissible under the terms of McCain-Feingold. In the House, two-thirds of successful 1994 challengers spent more than would have been allowed under the Smith-Shays proposal. Who knows how many of these challengers would have been successful had the regulators had their way.

The First Amendment

In addition to these strong policy reasons against increasing federal regulation of campaign financing, there is a very strong constitutional argument. The Supreme Court has held time and time again, from *Buckley vs. Valeo* in 1976 to last summer's *Colorado Republican* case [in 1996] that, in the context of campaign spending, *money equals speech.*

The protestations of Sen. Bill Bradley and Common Cause notwithstanding, the court merely employed common sense when it ruled in *Buckley* that "a restriction on the amount of money a person or group may spend on political communication during a campaign necessarily reduces the quantity of expression by restricting the number of issues discussed, the depth of their exploration, and the size of the audience." Attempts to limit how much money may be spent in a campaign are therefore unconstitutional abridgments of 1st Amendment rights of free speech. Much, if not all, of proposals such as McCain-Feingold and Smith-Shays would likely be held unconstitutional by the courts.

Many of those who advocate greater federal regulation, as well as those who advocate public financing of campaigns, must recognize the constitutional impediments to regulating free speech. As a result, they are now arguing that the 1st Amendment must be amended for the first time in history. And to what end? So that the federal government can tell individuals how much of their own money they are allowed to spend in elections.

While their goal is horrific—the American Civil Liberties Union (ACLU) called it "a recipe for repression"—proponents of a constitutional amendment have chosen an honest means. Amendment supporters are correct to note that what they want to accomplish cannot be done without such an amendment. But it is clearly a dangerous idea. The freedom of political speech is at the very heart of the 1st Amendment. To make an exception to the 1st Amendment for political speech would be to create an exception that renders the amendment as a whole largely meaningless.

Full Disclosure Is Sufficient

Campaign committees can and should be required to record contributions on a daily basis and to make that information immediately available over the Internet. The opposing campaign can be relied on to publicize any gift that can give rise to an adverse inference. The public can then judge whether the contribution is apt to corrupt its recipient.

The road to true reform lies not in trying to persuade the Supreme Court to permit further restrictions on political speech . . . but to persuade Congress to rescind those that now exist while requiring the immediate disclosure of contributions. We have nothing to fear from unfettered political debate, and everything to gain.

James L. Buckley, *National Review*, September 27, 1999.

A constitutional amendment would also be impossibly vague to enforce, particularly in the area of "issue advocacy" by groups ranging from the Christian Coalition to the AFL-CIO [labor organization]. Under current laws, such "issue advocacy," since it does not explicitly advocate the election or defeat of a particular candidate, falls beyond the parameters of federal election laws. But would a constitutional amendment drag it into the regulatory scheme? If not, then a constitutional amendment would effectively do nothing to stop campaign spending, since issue advocacy would then become the direction in which current expenditures would head.

I believe that these approaches—increasing regulation and amending the Constitution—are the wrong ones to take when it comes to fixing the problems that ail our campaign finance system. Instead, we should take a cue from the damage done by the regulations of the 1970s and adopt an approach that recognizes the complexity of the campaign finance system.

I think we should recognize that more money in campaigns means more democracy. It means more views will be heard, including those views we may find repugnant. Contribution limits are antithetical to the freedom we cherish in this country. As former Chief Justice Warren Burger wrote, "There are many prices we pay for freedoms secured by the 1st Amendment; the risk of undue influence is one of them, confirming what we have long known: Freedom is hazardous, but some restraints are worse."

No Limits and Full Disclosure

My proposal, the Citizen Legislature and Political Freedom Act, seeks to restore freedom to the process of electing leaders. Specifically, it will lift all limits on contributions to candidates so that Americans are free to give as much or as little as they wish to the candidate of their choice. In turn, elected officials, once they are able to raise money in larger increments, will be able to spend more time governing and less time grubbing for money, which the American people (and politicians!) find so distasteful.

Lifting contribution limits is only one-half of the equation, however. The system of financing campaigns will not be truly free until the American people are empowered to make informed decisions about the candidates they vote for and the forces that may influence them. The key to such a system is full disclosure of campaign contributions. Full disclosure will enable voters to identify and understand the influences that may affect a certain candidate, and to vote accordingly.

Unlike the McCain-Feingold approach, my proposal asks that Congress do something it rarely considers: Trust the people. Instead of imposing new restrictions and limitations on American voters in the name of protecting them from the realities of modern politics, we should simply allow voters to gather the information they need to make smart decisions.

As Professor Larry Sabato, the highly regarded political scientist from the University of Virginia, wrote in his book,

Dirty Little Secrets, "Let a well-informed marketplace, rather than a committee of federal bureaucrats, be the judge of whether someone has accepted too much money from a particular interest group or spent too much to win an election."

An Ideal System

Our goal should be a campaign finance system in which any American can compete for and win elective office. An ideal system would allow voters to contribute freely to the candidate of their choice, but would make certain such contributions were voluntary. And finally, a healthy campaign finance system would require that candidates fully disclose their contribution sources so that voters can make informed decisions.

The big government approach to campaign finance reform, embodied by the McCain-Feingold and Smith-Shays proposals, has failed in the past and is bound to fail in the future because it rests on false assumptions. It will exacerbate, not solve, the problems with the current system. Worse yet, it will demand that Americans sacrifice constitutional liberties.

It is time for a new approach. By allowing challengers to raise the money they need to be competitive, by enabling American citizens to give as much as they choose to the candidates of their choice, and by requiring that candidates fully disclose contributions, the Citizen Legislature and Political Freedom Act will restore freedom and integrity to our system of financing campaigns.

"Politicians would be . . . challenged to come up with a convincing answer to this question: Why do you need to know the identity of your donors?"

Making Campaign Contributions Anonymous Can Prevent Political Corruption

Jack Hitt

Jack Hitt, a writer for the *New York Times Magazine* and other publications, argues that radical solutions might be necessary to limit the influence of special interest money in elections while maintaining a voter's right to give money to a candidate. In the following viewpoint, he describes a proposal by Yale University law professor Ian Ayres and Stanford University economist Jeremy Bulow in which all campaign donations would come in through a blind trust. People would still have the ability to contribute to like-minded candidates, but would not be in a position to claim credit and expect specific favors from them. Hitt compares this proposed reform to the secret ballot, a nineteenth-century political reform that also was made to combat political corruption.

As you read, consider the following questions:

1. What fundamental paradoxical challenge lies at the heart of campaign finance reform, according to Hitt?
2. What practices were ended by adopting the secret ballot in voting, according to the author?
3. What are some of the possible ramifications of making political donations anonymous, in Hitt's opinion?

George W. Bush Jr. has raised the most money of any Presidential candidate in history: $36 million and counting. Much of it was gathered by only 200 people, super-fund-raisers whom Bush has dubbed "Pioneers." Should Bush get elected President next year [2000], it is not caviling to say that those 200 people are more likely to get a phone call through, and possibly even get a favor returned, than, say, I will. So who are these very possibly special people? Bush's campaign advisers have decided it is not in our interest to know, and there is no legal means to compel them to tell.

Outrageous? Well, is it any more upsetting than Al Gore's notorious visit to the Buddhist temple? Or the afternoon in 1995 when Representative John Boehner of Ohio, the G.O.P. Conference chairman, was spotted on the House floor cheerfully tossing out checks from tobacco lobbyists like daisies? How about when Trent Lott and Bill Clinton conspired in a fit of midnight *fraternité* to sneak through a $50 billion tax loophole for the tobacco companies? Does *anyone* disagree that our campaign-finance system has lapsed into legalized corruption? . . .

A Complex Problem

Every poll taken reveals that voters strongly favor reform. But when pressed for details of what might work, folks appear overwhelmed by the complexity. It seems like some public policy Rubik's cube for think-tank nerds to solve, with all that talk of spending caps, soft-money restrictions, limits on political action committees and Federal Election Commission reporting requirements. Even most expert commentary is little more than frustration venting. In a recent Op-Ed article, [former senator and presidential candidate] George McGovern lamented the "vexing" problem of "big money in politics. Thoughtful members of both parties are stymied by this issue."

What everyone seems to agree on, and has for decades, is that the problem boils down to "too much money" and the solution unquestionably involves "restrictions" and "fuller disclosure."

Actually, not *everyone* agrees about this. There are other

would-be reformers out there who describe the problem differently. To see the world their way is to see the limitations of fixes inspired by conventional wisdom. And to see how a radically different solution might not only solve our predicament quite elegantly but also profoundly change the way elections are conducted in the process.

The current crop of labored patches to the system . . . is trying to end-run a 23-year-old Supreme Court decision [*Buckley vs. Valeo*] that reasonably warned reformers that the voters' right to give money to candidates is inextricably bound up with the voters' right to free speech, expression and peaceable assembly. The brain teaser is this: How do you allow voters to freely donate money to the candidates and parties without permitting the easy money of special interests to crowd the rest of us out? Or, vice versa, how do you restrict the special interests without hobbling the necessary expression of voters in a robust election? . . .

Prof. Ian Ayres of Yale and a co-author, Jeremy Bulow of Stanford, have published a law-review article detailing their idea to allow anybody or any institution to give as much campaign money as they want. But with one key proviso: the candidate cannot find out who the donors are.

All campaign donations would be funneled through a blind trust. The candidate still gets the money. He just can't know to whom he owes, or doesn't owe, a favor. Anyone could claim to be a donor with the same impunity that each of us can safely claim to have "voted" for the politician. This idea questions reform's most basic assumption—that more and fuller disclosure is the only answer. "Instead of limiting money," the authors write, "we might limit information."

The Secret Ballot

The constitutionality of such a plan would be difficult to question. It is modeled on something seemingly more fundamental than even free-speech concerns: the secret ballot. Just as a voter goes into a booth and votes secretly, the donor would go into what the authors call, metaphorically, a "donation booth" and donate. In both cases, the voters know for whom they voted (donated to), but the candidates do not. The Supreme Court would be hard pressed to explain why a secret ballot is constitutional and a secret donation is not. And politicians would be equally challenged to come up with a convincing answer to this question: Why do you need to know the identity of your donors?

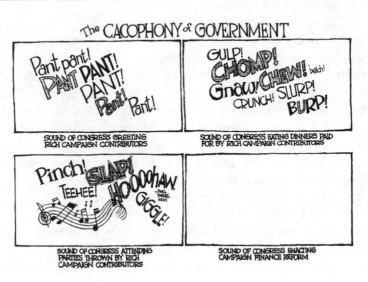

The CACOPHONY of GOVERNMENT

Pant pant! PANT PANT! PANT! Pant! Pant!

SOUND OF CONGRESS GREETING RICH CAMPAIGN CONTRIBUTORS

GULP! CHOMP! Gnaw! CHEW! belch! CRUNCH! SLURP! BURP!

SOUND OF CONGRESS EATING DINNERS PAID FOR BY RICH CAMPAIGN CONTRIBUTORS

Pinch! SLAP! TEEHEE! HOOOOHAW GIGGLE!

SOUND OF CONGRESS ATTENDING PARTIES THROWN BY RICH CAMPAIGN CONTRIBUTORS

SOUND OF CONGRESS ENACTING CAMPAIGN FINANCE REFORM

It turns out the secret ballot was invented for the precise reason the authors suggest the donation booth. In the 19th century, voting in America was shockingly corrupt. Party bosses organized voters and drove them to the voting stations like cattle. The ballots for opposing candidates were published on different colored paper. The bosses typically checked on their vote-buying by forcing voters into single-file lines and demanding that they physically wave their paid-for ballots over their heads. This practice came to an end when the "Australian ballot"—the secret ballot was invented there—came to America. Massachusetts was the first state to adopt the secret ballot, in 1888. South Carolina was the last . . . in 1950.

By and large, the secret ballot pretty much eliminated vote-buying; perhaps a donation booth would have a similar effect. It neatly solves the political action committee (PAC)

problem, which is a dark mutation of mandatory disclosure. Today, the PAC can "bundle" bags of legal checks for the candidates and explain precisely where they came from. With donation booths, PAC's would wither.

So, perhaps, would a lot of campaign contributions. After the secret ballot went into effect, voting dropped off nearly 7 percent. The authors themselves worry that their reform would "shift money toward less accountable 'issue advocacy' expenditures and may be so effective in disrupting the market for influence that it cripples candidates' ability to raise funds."

Just how far you think donations might plunge is almost a Rorschach test of how deeply corrupt you believe the system to be. I don't know about you, but I am comforted by the fact that voting fell only 7 percent. Would donations dip only a bit, suggesting that most contributors want little more than the election of a generally like-minded individual? Or would they crash, revealing that donors want specific quid pro quo, or nothing? Either outcome of the donation booth would be radical, in the sense that it would completely upend the system we currently have in place. But would anyone really miss it?

Perhaps the candidates would just become shuttlecocks battered amid a riot of citizen-financed issue ads. Would that be so bad? And if candidates could not afford to saturate television with either feel-good commercials, Vaselined with slo-mo family values or with negative ads predicting moral decay in stentorian voice-over, perhaps they would have to work the streets for votes and fashion clever speeches to attract free media exposure.

It would be utopian to think that any of these solutions would restore us to some Jeffersonian democracy of high-minded yeomen. (That never existed anyway.) But now we tolerate a system in which we routinely hear stories about, say, the presence of corporate campaign donors at Congressional staff meetings to draw up new environmental laws. In a truly transformed system, it just might be that our politicians would, from time to time, find themselves contemplating the affairs of their voters as a coherent whole instead of the concerns of their most generous fund-raisers. Imagine that.

"Ultimately, the only true campaign reform is to shrink government."

Shrinking the Size of the Federal Government Can Prevent Political Corruption

Doug Bandow

Doug Bandow is a columnist, television commentator, and senior fellow at the Cato Institute, a libertarian think tank. In the following viewpoint, he argues that there is much to criticize about how campaign contributions are solicited (he especially excoriates President Bill Clinton). However, he expresses skepticism about existing and proposed campaign financing rules, asserting that they could jeopardize freedom of speech and would not eliminate the influence of special interest groups. The only long-term solution, he argues, is to shrink the role and economic influence of government, thus ending the motivation of individuals and groups to attempt to manipulate government elections and policy for their own ends.

As you read, consider the following questions:
1. What comparison does Bandow make between the actions of the Republican congressional leadership and the administration of President Bill Clinton?
2. What problems does the author foresee with the public financing of campaigns?
3. How have the 1974 reforms helped political incumbents, according to Bandow?

Excerpted from Doug Bandow, "Meaningful Campaign Reform Needed," *Cato This Just In*, May 21, 1997. Reprinted by permission of the Cato Institute, Washington, D.C.

I s there anything the Clinton administration wouldn't sell in exchange for campaign contributions? Overnight stays in the Lincoln Bedroom, presidential photo opportunities, White House coffees, and all manner of "access" were available at a price. It turns out the Democrats seemingly placed federal policy on the auction block as well.

The Cheyenne-Arapaho Indians from Oklahoma donated $107,000 from a tribal welfare fund to the Democratic National Committee. In return they got lunch with President Clinton, two meetings with Vice President Gore, and what they believed was a promise for the return of tribal land from the federal government. The latter went unfilled, however. So Party officials suggested that the tribe chip in thousands more and hire a Democratic lobbyist.

The administration has long illustrated the meaning of the word "shameless," but every day Clinton and company seem to fall to new depths of sleaze. When confronted with each additional misdeed, the president dodges responsibility, declaring that he's for "campaign finance reform."

Of course, Republicans vigorously raise money from a variety of sources. But it is not the Republican National Committee that has had to return millions of dollars in tainted and possibly illegal contributions.

It's not the Republican congressional leadership that has consorted with a bevy of crooks, convicted felons, and even a foreign arms merchant. It's not top Republicans who have raised money from government offices, shaking down most any person or organization with business in Washington. . . .

Still, there is something to be said for campaign finance reform. The current system is obviously broken. Candidates never stop raising money. Groups and parties can spend as much as they want independently. Outsiders need to be wealthy to hope for success. Business groups give to everyone in hopes of preserving "access" with whomever wins.

Making a Bad System Worse

However, the usual reform proposals would make a bad system worse. The most important issue is constitutional: the First Amendment guarantees free speech, and nowhere is speech more important than in the electoral process. Yet, opines House Minority Leader Richard Gephardt, D-Missouri, "What we have is two important values in direct conflict: freedom of speech and our desire for healthy campaigns in a healthy democracy. You can't have both."

But how can one have "healthy campaigns in a healthy democracy" without protecting freedom of speech?

Public financing and tax-paid support for advertising, postage and travel would force voters to underwrite candidates who they oppose. Cheap or free broadcasting for candidates would effectively nationalize the private media—without eliminating the current bias against third-party candidates. Limitations on independent activity are potentially broad enough to restrict letters to the editor; even more modest rules would hamper electoral activism by individuals and groups.

The Biggest Growth Factor

The biggest growth factor in scandal politics has been the growth of federal power in Washington, particularly via the less-accountable regulatory state. With more at stake in every decision involving taxes, spending, and regulation, special interests necessarily find lobbying and influence peddling more attractive. If you build increased opportunities to pick other people's pockets and gain special advantages, they will come—in very nice suits, with business cards. You get the metastasizing growth of the whole parasite culture of lobbyists, trade associations, journalists, lawyers, and talking heads.

That in turn makes the public suspicious that, despite all the technical ethics-based formalities on the surface, there has to be a great amount of questionable wheeling and dealing just outside the official spotlight.

Tom Miller, *CEI Update*, October 1997.

Nor would any of these supposed fixes eliminate the influence of powerful interest groups. Rather, such changes would merely enhance the power of one faction (say, labor unions) to the detriment of another (perhaps trade associations). In fact, it was the campaign reform law of 1974 that, by outlawing large contributions, spurred the development of political action committees.

What happened over the past two decades? PAC outlays jumped eightfold. Campaign spending increased by more than 350 percent.

Even more disturbing is how the 1974 "reforms" reinforced incumbents. According to Bradley Smith of Capital University Law School, "House incumbents, who had previously outspent challengers by approximately 1.5 to 1, now outspend challengers by nearly 4 to 1; incumbent re-election rates have risen to record high levels." Almost all current reform proposals would similarly aid incumbents.

The Only True Reform

Ultimately, the only true campaign reform is to shrink government. As long as $1.7 trillion in taxpayer wealth is available for plundering in Washington, interest groups will spend hundreds of millions of dollars to get their hands on it. As long as a federal bureaucrat's whim can disable or enrich entire industries, individuals, associations, unions and corporations will manipulate the political process for their own ends.

In the meantime, Congress should deregulate elections. Allow any contribution of any amount, so long as it is fully disclosed. This would end the all-consuming search to skirt the law. It would ensure the fullest participation of all Americans in politics. And it would let voters, who could judge the candidates' fund-raising practices as well as policy positions, have the final say.

| "*If we fail to craft a workable substiute to the independent counsel, down the road we'll find ourselves in a crisis.*"

The Independent Counsel Law Should Be Reformed

Joseph I. Lieberman

The 1978 Ethics in Government Act, passed four years after the Watergate scandal, authorized the use of special prosecutors appointed by a panel of federal judges to investigate allegations of misconduct by the president and other high government officials. Over the next two decades at least twenty investigations were performed by such special prosecutors, renamed independent counsels in 1983. Some of the investigations were highly controversial—including Kenneth W. Starr's probe on President Bill Clinton that began in 1994— and have led some observers to conclude that the independent counsel statute was fatally flawed. In the following viewpoint, written several months before the law authorizing independent counsels was to expire in June 1999, Senator Joseph I. Lieberman of Delaware argues that while the statute may need to be changed in minor ways, such laws are still needed to assure the public that scandalous conduct by high officials will be fully and independently investigated. Lieberman, a Democrat, was first elected to the U.S. Senate in 1988.

As you read, consider the following questions:
1. What changes in the independent counsel statute does Lieberman suggest?
2. What will happen if the independent counsel statute is terminated, according to the author?

Reprinted from Joseph I. Lieberman, "Mend, Don't End, the Counsel Law," *Newsday*, March 12, 1999, by permission of the author.

Twenty years ago [in 1978], a reform-minded Congress, shaken by the jarring experience of Watergate, approved a series of laws that began a new era of government accountability. One, the independent-counsel statute, was meant to reassure a skeptical public that criminal investigations of those at the highest levels of power would be insulated from the political influence of the very people under suspicion.

At the time, the memory of Richard Nixon's firing of [special prosecutor] Archibald Cox five years earlier was fresh and seemed reason enough for the statute. That episode had launched a profound constitutional crisis and demonstrated just how far one president was prepared to go to stop an investigation of his administration. Now, the bitter controversies surrounding the work of independent counsels Lawrence Walsh [investigator of Iran-Contra] and Kenneth W. Starr [Bill Clinton investigator] appear to have created a bipartisan coalition to terminate the law.

A Crisis in Public Confidence

But if two decades have taken their toll on the independent-counsel statute, the underlying principle remains as powerful as ever, perhaps more so. Public confidence in government is severely depressed. Cynicism and doubt fueled by warring political parties and divided government are epidemic. And the most damning evidence is plainly before us: Voting is at its lowest level in half a century, ranking the United States 137th out of 163 world democracies in voter participation. This seems a poor time to kill a statute that can sustain what faith the public still has left in honest, accountable government.

The independent-counsel statute should be changed to reflect what 20 years has taught us, for at times it seems to have become a vehicle for, rather than a protection against, the abuse of power. But the value of an executive branch investigator protected from conflicts of interest and political influence is still too essential to relinquish.

So what should be done? An independent-counsel law is most effective when used for significant investigations and least effective when used to pursue flimsy charges. To limit use of the law, Congress might raise the evidentiary threshold for appointing an independent counsel and reduce the number of executive branch officials—now 240—who fall under its jurisdiction.

⌐Necessary for Extreme Cases

The independent counsel statute should be reserved for those extreme crises in American government—such as Watergate, Teapot Dome, and a handful of others—that require a fail-safe mechanism to deal with percolating crises in government. The statute would be constrained in this fashion by retooling the triggering mechanism; sharply narrowing the category of individuals and offenses covered; reining in the special prosecutor and controlling his or her jurisdiction; restoring more power to the Justice Department; and spelling out the special court's duties so that it could intelligently monitor cases. The statute would thus become a back-up mechanism, to deal with the infrequent case in which a) serious allegations of criminal wrongdoing at the top of the Executive Branch surfaced; b) those charges were well-developed; and c) a presumption was met that the Executive Branch would not be capable of conducting a fair and neutral investigation of itself.

Kenneth Gormley, *Congressional Digest*, 1999.

As the law now stands, the attorney general must request an independent counsel if there are "reasonable grounds to believe that further investigation is warranted." Perhaps that hair-trigger threshold should be raised to "probable cause" or "reasonable grounds to believe a crime has been committed."

Limiting the Scope of Investigations

We might also consider limitations on an independent counsel's ability to expand his or her jurisdiction beyond the scope of the original investigation. The statute now requires the attorney general to give "great weight" to such a recommendation and to reach a decision within 30 days.

This permits an independent counsel to leapfrog from one matter to the next—witness Starr's progression from investigating Whitewater to Travelgate to Filegate to Monica Lewinsky—in essence becoming the president's permanent personal inquisitor. One solution would be for the statute instead to establish a presumption against expansion of jurisdiction and require appointment of a separate independent counsel if evidence of additional criminal behavior by the same subject of an investigation surfaces.

Perhaps we might decide to establish a special office within the Department of Justice. The office might be headed by a public prosecutor who is confirmed by the Senate but who would be protected from summary dismissal by the attorney general to guarantee his or her independence.

These are just a smattering of the ideas that have been floated in answer to the many critics who question the sweeping powers ceded to independent counsels over the years. But they are ideas bred from 20 years of experience and built on the admirable service records of most of the independent counsels, who, not coincidentally, have been neither controversial nor well known.

A Bedrock Principle

I have no doubt that if we fail to craft a workable substitute to the independent counsel, down the road we'll find ourselves in a crisis similar to Watergate or Iran-contra or Whitewater, with a public skeptical of the legitimacy of the criminal process and, possibly, with a president or attorney general more interested in his or her own career than in getting to the facts.

Then, we will wish that in 1999 we had done more to preserve the bedrock democratic principle of the rule of law, that is, the ability to independently prosecute even our most powerful officeholders.

"Noble in concept, and grounded in the principle of equal justice under law, the statute has, sadly, failed to live up to the ideals which caused its creation."

The Independent Counsel Act Should Be Allowed to Expire

Philip S. Anderson

Philip S. Anderson is president of the American Bar Association, a private organization of the nation's lawyers. The following viewpoint is excerpted from congressional testimony describing the ABA's position on the independent counsel statute, which was up for reauthorization. Anderson argues that while the ABA previously supported the creation of independent counsels to investigate government corruption, it now has concluded that such a statute creates more problems than it solves. The concept of independent counsels is flawed, he contends, because of their total lack of accountability and their ability to pursue open-ended investigations of relatively trivial matters that violate the civil rights of those being investigated. Cases of possible corruption of high government officials can be handled by special prosecutors appointed by the attorney general, Anderson concludes. Congress ultimately agreed to let the statute expire in June 1999.

As you read, consider the following questions:
1. How has the ABA's position on independent counsels evolved since 1978, according to Anderson?
2. What five fundamental flaws of the statute does the author identify?

Excerpted from Philip S. Anderson's statement before the House Committee on the Judiciary, Subcommittee on Commercial and Administrative Law, March 10, 1999.

I am Philip S. Anderson, President of the American Bar Association. I am pleased to . . . express the views of our Association with respect to the Independent Counsel statute.

In the wake of Watergate, we created a high-level committee to study how to insulate federal law enforcement processes from improper influences. In 1976 the committee issued its findings, including a set of 20 recommendations for preventing improper influences on the Department of Justice, the Federal Bureau of Investigation, and the Internal Revenue Service. Included among the 20 recommendations was one opposing a permanent office of special prosecutor but recommending a mechanism by which a special prosecutor could be appointed when conflicts of interest or appearances of impropriety would make it inappropriate for the Attorney General and the prosecutors within the Department of Justice to handle a particular matter. The Association's recommendation of this triggering mechanism played a significant role in the enactment in 1978 of the special prosecutor (now independent counsel) provisions of the Ethics in Government Act.

A Change of Opinion

In February 1999 at our Midyear Meeting, our House of Delegates, by a vote of 384 to 49, adopted the following resolutions on this subject:

RESOLVED, that the American Bar Association opposes reauthorization of the Independent Counsel provisions of the Ethics in Government Act (hereinafter called "Independent Counsel Act") in any form. . . .

Why has the Association now abandoned its original view of the need for such a statute and recommended its demise? The central motivation of our 1976 policy was to address concerns about public confidence in the justice system in cases involving high-level Executive Branch officials. As stated in the report which accompanied the 1976 recommendations, ". . . the public must be assured that crimes committed in high places will be investigated and prosecuted fearlessly and with integrity."

It has become all too clear that, since its 1978 enactment, the statute no longer assures such public confidence. The public clearly believes that, rather than ensuring that all people are treated equally before the law, the statute has caused those subject to its purview to be treated in a far more hostile and unbalanced way.

The Association did not come to its present view suddenly or lightly. On three prior occasions (1982, 1987 and 1993), our House of Delegates adopted recommendations for significant amendments to the statute to address notable problems and defects which had become evident. For example, our 1982 policy—adopted barely four years after the statute's enactment—recommended ten separate amendments to the statute. Among them were recommendations to limit the crimes which could trigger the appointment of a special prosecutor to a specified few; to limit the high officials covered by the statute; and to require the special prosecutor to adhere to the formal prosecutorial guidelines of the Department of Justice. . . .

Defects of the Statute

By 1999, however, those who had studied the operation of the statute concluded it was so seriously flawed that it should be allowed to die. Among the defects in the statute which have been identified are the following:

1. The Act fails to insure meaningful accountability of an Independent Counsel to the electorate or any other effective supervisory authority.

2. The Act results in the investigation and sometimes in the prosecution of matters that are trivial or innocuous and that would not have resulted in action by the Department of Justice but for the rigid requirements of the Act. Ironically, the Act was intended to assure that "covered persons" were treated like ordinary citizens in terms of investigation and prosecution, but the mandatory nature of the statute results in covered persons being denied basic protections—e.g., secrecy that an investigation is underway—that other citizens routinely rely upon.

3. The Act poses a grave danger that an Independent Counsel, assigned with the task of investigating one person, will lose perspective and will view any instance of alleged misconduct as requiring the attention of fed-

eral law enforcement, even if such misconduct would be ignored were it called to the attention of a typical federal prosecutor.

4. The Act poses a danger that open-ended investigations, with neither time nor budgetary limitations, will result in expenditures of vast sums of taxpayer money to investigate minor matters, and that targets of an Independent Counsel's investigation will be required to mortgage their lives in response.

5. The Act creates dual responsibilities for an Independent Counsel—to do what an ordinary prosecutor is expected to do, and to complete a report explaining all events investigated which no ordinary prosecutor ever does. The conflict between investigating and prosecuting, on the one hand, and creating an historical record, on the other hand, is real and in some instances is sufficient to guarantee that investigations of minor matters will be lengthy, expensive, and disruptive.

Noble in concept, and grounded in the principle of equal justice under law, the statute has, sadly, failed to live up to the ideals which caused its creation. The problem is not that

Ben Sargent. Copyright ©1999 Austin American Statesman. Reprinted by permission of Universal Press Syndicate. All rights reserved.

the men and women appointed to serve as Independent Counsels lack talent or judgment; the problem is that they are given an assignment that too often appears to be the investigation of an individual rather than a crime. . . .

If Congress concludes, as we have, that the statute is so flawed it should not be reauthorized, the question remains of how allegations against high-ranking officials should be handled. Other existing laws and Department of Justice regulations permit the Attorney General to appoint a Special Counsel to act in matters where the public confidence will be materially benefited by having an independent person in charge of the investigation. This procedure was used for the engagement of Archibald Cox and his successor, Leon Jaworski; it was used to appoint Paul Curran to investigate the allegations regarding President Carter's peanut warehouse; it was used to appoint Robert Fiske, who was the first person appointed to look into the Whitewater matter. It has also been used for matters that would not have been covered by the Independent Counsel Act, such as the investigation of the allegations concerning misuse of the bank at the U.S. House of Representatives by some members of Congress. In each instance, the Special Counsel conducted successful investigations in a responsible manner that preserved public confidence.

Periodical Bibliography

The following articles have been selected to supplement the diverse views presented in this chapter. Addresses are provided for periodicals not indexed in the *Readers' Guide to Periodical Literature*, the *Alternative Press Index*, the *Social Sciences Index*, or the *Index to Legal Periodicals and Books*.

Ian Ayres and Jeremy Bulow	"The Donation Booth: Mandating Donor Anonymity to Disrupt the Market for Political Influence," *Stanford Law Review*, Fall 1998.
Bobby Birchfield	"Enemies of the First Amendment," *Weekly Standard*, October 11, 1999.
James L. Buckley	"Bucks and Buckley," *National Review*, September 27, 1999.
Archibald Cox and Philip B. Heynman	"After the Counsel Law," *New York Times*, March 10, 1999.
Joseph E. DiGenova	"The Independent Counsel Act: A Good Time to End a Bad Idea," *Georgetown Law Journal*, July 1998.
E.J. Dionne Jr.	"Campaign Spending," *Commonweal*, September 24, 1999.
Bob Dole and George J. Mitchell	"It's Not the Job, but How It's Filled," *New York Times*, May 17, 1999.
Journal of Legislation	"Campaign Finance Reform Symposium," vol. 24, no. 2, 1998.
Robert Kuttner	"Rescuing Democracy from Speech," *American Prospect*, January/February 1998.
Thomas E. Mann	"Deregulating Campaign Finance," *Brookings Review*, Winter 1998.
John McCain	"Campaign-Finance Reform Is Right for Conservatives," *Wall Street Journal*, October 14, 1999.
Ellen S. Miller	"Clean Elections, How To," *American Prospect*, January/February 1997.
Bill Moyers	"Hostile Takeover," *Sojourners*, July/August 1998.
Viveca Novak	"Dialing Back the Dollars," *Time*, September 6, 1999.
Jonathan Rauch	"Give Pols Free Money, No Rules," *U.S. News & World Report*, December 29, 1997.
Henry Ruth	"The Case for Independent Counsels," *Wall Street Journal*, March 1, 1999.
William Safire	"After Indy Counsels," *New York Times*, March 4, 1999.

For Further Discussion

Chapter 1

1. Martin L. Gross argues that criminal behavior is rife in American politics, while Anthony Lewis contends that innocent people are victimized by scandal investigations and the media. What specific examples does each author provide in support of their general thesis? Which do you find more convincing?

2. Richard N. Goodwin and Martin L. Gross both make the argument that that campaign contributions to politicians are equivalent to bribes, while Michael Barone argues that they are examples of people exercising their First Amendment right to free speech. In your opinion, in what circumstances does a political contribution qualify as a legitimate form of speech, and in what contexts might it be considered a bribe?

3. Anthony Lewis and Richard N. Goodwin both cite James Madison, America's fourth president and one of the principal creators of the U.S. constitution, in making their arguments. Do you believe the ideas of Madison and his contemporaries still have relevance in examining the problems of contemporary American politics? Why or why not?

Chapter 2

1. Leslie Carbone argues that "character counts" in political leadership. Do you agree or disagree? If you disagree, does that mean you believe that "character doesn't count"? Does John B. Judis make this argument? Explain.

2. Leslie Carbone and Gary L. Bauer both have past and present affiliations with the Family Research Council, a group associated with the Christian right. Defenders of the religious right argue that they are defending traditional American values against attack, while critics have accused them of trying to impose their own views of morality on others. Is either position evident in Carbone and Bauer's arguments on Bill Clinton and morality? Does it affect how you receive their arguments? Explain how.

3. Michael Walzer presents certain values he expects politicians to uphold. Is his list complete, in your opinion? What other attributes would you want to see in your political leaders? What other attributes might Armstrong Williams, Patrick McCormick, and other authors in this chapter want to add?

Chapter 3

1. Jerrold Nadler argues that the purpose of impeachment is to protect the nation, not to punish the president. Does the House Judiciary Committee accept or reject this premise? In your view, would accepting Nadler's assertion strengthen or weaken the case for impeaching Bill Clinton? Explain your answer.

2. After reading the viewpoints of Eric Pooley and David Frum, list what you feel are the closest parallels between the Lewinsky scandal and Watergate. Then list what you believe to be the biggest differences. After reviewing the lists, decide whether you agree or disagree with Frum that "the Lewinsky scandal is almost eerily like Watergate." Defend your answer.

3. Among the words Robert H. Bork uses to describe Clinton and his administration are "pathological," "squalid," "outrageous," and "sexually depraved." Do you think these were used as part of reasoned arguments or as inflammatory language designed to appeal to emotion? Explain. Can you find different examples of potentially inflammatory words in Bork's article?

4. Does Robert Parry defend Clinton's actions beyond attacking his political opponents? Do you think his analysis of the Clinton scandals was an effective and adequate defense of the president's behavior? Why or why not?

Chapter 4

1. Which of the "four false assumptions" that John Doolittle says are held by campaign finance reform advocates can you find expressed in the viewpoints of John B. Judis and the Committee for Economic Development? Which, if any, of the four claims do you agree with Doolittle to be erroneous? Which, if any, do you think have validity despite Doolittle's arguments? Explain your answer.

2. Do you think Jack Hitt's proposed anonymous "donation booth" is practical? Can you anticipate any potential problems in implementing his proposal? Explain.

3. What fundamental defects of the independent counsel statute justify its expiration, according to the ABA? Does Joseph Lieberman adequately address these concerns in his proposed modifications of the law? Why or why not?

Organizations to Contact

The editors have compiled the following list of organizations concerned with the issues debated in this book. The descriptions are derived from materials provided by the organizations. All have publications or information available for interested readers. The list was compiled on the date of publication of the present volume; the information provided here may change. Be aware that many organizations take several weeks or longer to respond to inquiries, so allow as much time as possible.

Accuracy in Media (AIM)
4455 Connecticut Ave. NW, Suite 330, Washington, DC 20008
(202) 364-4401 • fax: (202) 364-4098
e-mail: info@aim.org • website: www.aim.org/
AIM is a conservative watchdog organization. It researches public complaints on errors of fact made by the news media and requests that the errors be corrected publicly. It publishes the bimonthly *AIM Report* and a weekly syndicated newspaper column.

American Civil Liberties Union (ACLU)
125 Broad St., 18th Floor, New York, NY 10004
(212) 549-2500 • fax: (212) 549-2646
website: www.aclu.org
The ACLU is a national organization that works to defend Americans' civil rights as guaranteed by the U.S. Constitution. It has opposed limits on political campaign contributions on the grounds that such restrictions violate the First Amendment. The ACLU publishes and distributes policy statements, pamphlets, and the semiannual newsletter *Civil Liberties Alert*.

American Enterprise Institue for Public Policy Research (AEI)
1150 17th St. NW, Washington, DC 20036
(202) 862-5800 fax: (202) 862-7177
e-mail: dmaxwell@aei.org • website: www.aei.org
AEI is a conservative think tank that studies such issues as government regulation, religion, philosophy, and legal policy. AEI's publications include books as well as the bimonthly magazine the *American Enterprise*.

Brookings Institution
1775 Massachusetts Ave. NW, Washington, DC 20036
(202) 797-6000 fax: (202) 797-6004
website: www.brook.edu

Founded in 1927, the institution is a liberal research and education organization that publishes material on economics, government, and foreign policy. It strives to serve as a bridge between scholarship and public policy, bringing new knowledge to the attention of decision makers and providing scholars with improved insight into public policy issues. Its publications include the quarterly *Brookings Review* and *Campaign Finance Reform: A Sourcebook*.

Cato Institute
1000 Massachusetts Ave. NW, Washington, DC 20001-5403
(202) 842-0200 • fax: (202) 842-3490
e-mail: cato@cato.org • website: www.cato.org

The Cato Institute is a libertarian public policy research foundation dedicated to limiting the control of government and protecting individual liberties. It offers numerous publications on public policy issues, including the triennial *Cato Journal*, the bimonthly newsletter *Cato Policy Report*, and the quarterly magazine *Regulation*.

Center for Public Integrity (CPI)
910 17th St. NW, 7th Floor, Washington, DC 20006
(202) 466-1300 • fax: (202) 466-1101
website: www.publicintegrity.org

The center is a nonprofit organization that examines ethics-related issues in government. It publishes numerous studies and reports, including *The Buying of the President 2000*.

Center for Responsive Politics (CRP)
1320 19th St. NW, Suite 620, Washington, DC 20036
(202) 857-0044 • fax: (202) 857-7809
e-mail: info@crp.org • website: www.crp.org

The CRP is a private organization that tracks money in politics and its effect on public policy. It publishes the *Capital Eye* newsletter and numerous reports. Its website also provides detailed information on funding sources for presidential and congressional incumbents and challengers.

The Century Foundation
41 E. 70th St., New York, NY 10021
(212) 535-4441 • fax: (212) 535-7534
e-mail: info@tcf.org • website: www.tcf.org

This research foundation, formerly known as the Twentieth Century Fund, sponsors analysis of economic policy, foreign affairs, and domestic political issues. It publishes numerous books and reports including *Buckley Stops Here: Loosening the Judicial Stranglehold on Campaign Finance Reform*.

Christian Coalition (CC)
1801-L Sara Dr., Chesapeake, VA 23320
(804) 424-2630 • fax: (804) 434-9068
e-mail: coalition@cc.org • website: www.cc.org

Founded by evangelist Pat Robertson, the coalition is a grassroots political organization of Christian fundamentalists working to elect moral legislators and stop what it believes is the moral decay of government. Its publications include the monthly newsletter *The Religious Right Watch* and the monthly tabloid *Christian American*.

Common Cause
1250 Connecticut Ave. NW, Suite 600, Washington, DC 20036
(202) 833-1200
website: www.commoncause.org

Common Cause is a liberal lobbying organization that works to improve the ethical standards of Congress and government in general. Its priorities include campaign finance reform, making government officials accountable for their actions, and promoting civil rights for all citizens. Common Cause publishes the quarterly *Common Cause Magazine* as well as position papers and reports.

Democratic National Committee (DNC)
430 S. Capitol St. SE, Washington, DC 20003
(202) 863-8000
website: www.democrats.org

The DNC formulates and promotes policies and positions of the Democratic Party. Its website includes information on party activities and campaigns.

Family Research Council (FRC)
700 13th St. NW, Suite 500, Washington, DC 20005
(202) 393-2100 • fax: (202) 393-2134
The council is a research, resource, and education organization that promotes the traditional family, which it defines as a group of people bound by marriage, blood, or adoption. The council publishes numerous reports from a conservative perspective, including the monthly newsletter *Washington Watch*.

Federal Election Commission (FEC)
999 E St. NW, Washington, DC 20463
(800) 424-9530
website: www.fec.gov
The FEC is an independent regulatory agency created by Congress in 1975 to adminster the Federal Election Campaign Act (FECA). It oversees public funding of presidential elections and enforces campaign finance laws. Its website includes financial disclosure reports and data about national election campaigns.

Heritage Foundation
214 Massachusetts Ave. NE, Washington, DC 20002-4999
(202) 546-4400 • fax: (202) 546-8328
e-mail: info@heritage.org • website: www.heritage.org
The foundation is a public policy research institute that advocates limited government and the free market system. It believes the private sector, not government, should be relied upon to ease social problems. The Heritage Foundation publishes the quarterly *Policy Review*, as well as hundreds of monographs, books, and background papers.

Judicial Watch
PO Box 44444, Washington, DC 20026
(888) 593-8442 • fax: (202) 646-5199
e-mail: info@judicialwatch.org • website: www.judicialwatch.org
Judicial Watch is a nonpartisan conservative foundation meant to serve as a "watchdog" against corrupt practices and ethical and legal transgressions in the federal government. It has brought several lawsuits against the administration of President Bill Clinton for what it considers to be scandalous acts of misconduct and betrayal of the public trust, including illegal campaign fundraising. Its website provides information about the cases the organization is involved in.

League of Women Voters
1730 M St. NW, Suite 1000, Washington, DC 20036-4508
(202) 429-1965 • fax: (202) 429-0854
website: www.lwv.org

The League of Women Voters is a private nonpartisan political organization that works to encourage an informed and active participation of citizens in government. It provides informational materials and position papers on voter participation and campaign finance on its website.

The Pew Research Center for the People and the Press
1150 18th St., NW, Suite 975, Washington, DC 20036
(202) 293-3126 • fax: (202) 293-2569
website: www.people-press.org

Formerly known as the *Times Mirror* Center for the People and the Press, the organization is an independent opinion research group that studies attitudes toward press, politics and public policy issues. Results of its surveys are freely available on its website.

Public Campaign
1320 19th St. NW, Suite M-1, Washington, DC 20036
(202) 293-0222 • fax: (202) 293-0202
e-mail: mengle@publicampaign.org
website: www.publicampaign.org

Public Campaign is a nonpartisan campaign finance reform organization that seeks to reduce the role of special interest money in American politics. It publishes educational materials on various campaign reform measures and provides news, polling data, and commentary on money in politics on its website.

Republican National Committee (RNC)
310 First St. SE, Washington, DC 20003
(202) 863-8500 • fax: (202) 863-8820
e-mail: info@rnc.org • website: www.rnc.org

The RNC formulates and promotes policies and positions of the Republican Party. Its website includes information on party activities and campaigns.

Bibliography of Books

Frank Anechiarico and James B. Jacobs — *The Pursuit of Absolute Integrity: How Corruption Control Makes Government Ineffective.* Chicago: University of Chicago Press, 1996.

William J. Bennett — *The Death of Outrage: Bill Clinton and the Assault on American Ideals.* New York: Free, 1998.

David Burnham — *Above the Law: Secret Deals, Political Fixes, and Other Misadventures of the U.S. Department of Justice.* New York: Scribner, 1996.

James Carville — *. . . And the Horse You Rode in On: The People v. Kenneth Starr.* New York: Simon & Schuster, 1998.

Alexander Cockburn and Ken Silverstein — *Washington Babylon.* New York: Verso, 1996.

Gail Collins — *Scorpion Tongues: Gossip, Celebrity, and American Politics.* New York: William Morrow, 1998.

Anthony Corrado, ed. — *Campaign Finance Reform: A Sourcebook.* Washington, DC: Brookings Institution, 1997.

Ann H. Coulter — *High Crimes and Misdemeanors: The Case Against Bill Clinton.* Washington, DC: Regnery, 1998.

Alan M. Dershowitz — *Sexual McCarthyism: Clinton, Starr, and the Emerging Constitutional Crisis.* New York: BasicBooks, 1998.

Elizabeth Drew — *The Corruption of American Politics: What Went Wrong and Why.* New York: Birch Lane, 1999.

Fred Emery — *Watergate: The Corruption and Fall of Richard Nixon.* London: Jonathan Cape, 1994.

James Fallows — *Breaking the News: How the Media Undermine American Democracy.* New York: Pantheon, 1996.

Suzanne Garment — *Scandal: The Crisis of Mistrust in American Politics.* New York: Times Books, 1991.

Benjamin Ginsberg and Martin Shefter — *Politics by Other Means.* New York: W.W. Norton, 1999.

Robert K. Goidel, Donald A. Gross, and Todd G. Shields — *Money Matters: Consequences of Campaign Finance Reform in the U.S. House Elections.* Lanham, MD: Rowman & Littlefield, 1999.

Linda R. Hirshman and Jane E. Larson — *Hard Bargains: The Politics of Sex.* New York: Oxford University Press, 1998.

Michael Isikoff — *Uncovering Clinton: A Reporter's Story.* New York: Crown, 1999.

Charles Lewis   *The Buying of the Congress: How Special Interests Have Stolen Your Right to Life, Liberty, and the Pursuit of Happiness.* New York: Avon, 1998.

Gene Lyons   *Fools for Scandal: How the Media Invented Whitewater.* New York: Franklin Square, 1996.

Eugene McCarthy   *No-Fault Politics: Modern Presidents, the Press, and Reformers.* New York: Times Books, 1998

Peter W. Morgan and Glenn H. Reynolds   *The Appearance of Impropriety: How Ethics Wars Have Undermined American Government, Business, and Society.* New York: Free, 1997.

Andrew Morton   *Monica's Story.* New York: St. Martin's, 1999.

Richard Posner   *An Affair of State: The Investigation, Impeachment, and Trial of President Clinton.* Cambridge, MA: Harvard University Press, 1999.

James D. Retter   *Anatomy of a Scandal: An Investigation into the Campaign to Undermine the Clinton Presidency.* Los Angeles: General, 1998.

E. Joshua Rosenkranz   *Buckley Stops Here: Loosening the Judicial Stranglehold on Campaign Finance Reform.* New York: Century Foundation, 1998.

Larry J. Sabato and Glenn R. Simpson   *Dirty Little Secrets: The Persistence of Corruption in American Politics.* New York: Times Books, 1996.

James B. Stewart   *Blood Sport: The President and His Adversaries.* New York: Simon & Schuster, 1996.

Dennis F. Thompson   *Ethics in Congress: From Individual to Institutional Corruption.* Washington, DC: Brookings Institution, 1995.

Edward Timperlake and William C. Triplett II   *Year of the Rat: How Bill Clinton Compromised U.S. Security for Chinese Cash.* Washington, DC: Regnery, 1998.

Jeffery Toobin   *A Vast Conspiracy: The Real Story of the Sex Scandal That Nearly Brought Down a President.* New York: Random House, 2000.

Gregory S. Walden   *On Best Behavior: The Clinton Administration and Ethics in Government.* Indianapolis: Hudson Institute, 1996.

Lawrence E. Walsh   *Firewall: The Iran-Contra Conspiracy and Cover-up.* New York: Norton, 1997.

Robert Williams   *Political Scandals in the USA.* Chicago: Fitzroy Dearborn, 1998.

J. Philip Wogaman   *From the Eye of the Storm.* Louisville, KY: Westminster John Knox, 1998.

Bob Woodward   *Shadow: Five Presidents and the Legacy of Watergate.* New York: Simon & Schuster, 1999.

Index